May 20, 1992

Dear Sherma,

Thank you for all your support in Keynotes this past year –

LESSONS FROM LIFE

LESSONS FROM LIFE
WAYNE B. LYNN

Bookcraft
Salt Lake City, Utah

Library of Congress Catalog Card Number: 87–71368
ISBN 0–88494–633–9

First Printing, 1987

Printed in the United States of America

Contents

Preface vii

I. Learning from Experience

1. Two Hundred Yards 3
2. Letting Go 5
3. True or False 9
4. The Day Our School Burned Down 12
5. Skin Your Own Skunks 17
6. Our Own Track 20
7. A Still Small Voice 23

II. Overcoming Obstacles

8. Young Courage 33
9. The Winter of Tribulation 40
10. Courage to Endure 43
11. A Different Kind of Courage 50
12. Free to Soar .53
13. To All the World 55

III. Working with Others

14. The Least Among Us 59
15. Of Foolish Ventures 62
16. A Better House 65

17. Where Would You Have Him Go?. 67
18. Look Not on His Countenance 71
19. The Truth Will Go Forth 74
20. Clogged Machines 76
21. The Boy Is Worth More Than the Cow 79
22. Only What You Give Away. 82
23. I Stand at the Door. 85
24. If the Trumpet Give an Uncertain Sound. 89
25. The Pay That Doesn't Come in an Envelope 92

Index 99

Preface

Our journey through life is not a well-marked path but one that confronts us daily with forks in the road requiring choices to be made. These choices are not always easy to make but give direction to our lives nevertheless.

I remember the counsel of my father suggesting that older folks could help guide youth down some roads since they had been over the road before.

More than one foolish venture caused me pain or embarrassment. While I was still figuratively dusting myself off my father would remark, "Now let that be a lesson to you."

This was sometimes said in humor but more often as sound advice. After all, isn't that what life is all about? We can't live long enough to make every mistake ourselves nor do we want to. Therefore, we try to learn from others.

I would like to dedicate this book to my father and to you, dear reader. As I share a few of life's experiences may you, "Let that be a lesson to you."

I. Learning from Experience

1

Two Hundred Yards

The horse he was riding was high strung and skittish. As he rode up alongside the barbed-wire fence approaching the wire gate, he tried to lean from his saddle and unfasten the loop from the gate pole to gain entry. Each time he leaned toward the gate his horse skittered sideways away from the fence, nearly dumping him from the saddle. In frustration he finally climbed down from the saddle and approached the gate. With both feet firmly planted on the ground and the reins held firmly in his hand, he tried once again to lift the wire loop.

Each time he gave a tug on the gate, his horse shied back, pulling at the reins in his hand and stretching his arm away from his task. He thought of dropping the reins to the ground but reconsidered, knowing the horse might bolt and leave him stranded out on the prairie.

Impulsively and in desperation, he gave the reins a quick wrap and tie around his leg. With his arms thus freed he easily opened the wire gate and gave it a high toss away from him so he could ride through without obstruction. When he threw the gate, his horse lifted his head high, his eyes glazed in terror. With one swift bound the horse was off and running, his head twisting sideways as he dragged his human cargo along. Over sage and hill, cactus, rocky ground, and rabbit brush they sailed with abandon.

In recounting the memorable event later to amused friends who were daubing iodine and extracting cactus thorns, the bruised cowboy was heard to observe philosophically, "You know, that horse hadn't dragged me moren' a couple hundred yards till I knew I had made a mistake!"

Life offers many such experiences from which we can grow wiser. Sometimes we are dragged less than "a couple hundred yards," while at other times we are dragged for miles before we recognize the error of our ways.

This little collection of homespun observations is intended to blend humor with wisdom in the hope that while being entertained, the reader may also discover some applications to himself that will make life easier to live, or at least easier to understand.

2

Letting Go

I was sitting on the floor next to the door taking up as little room as possible, my arms locked around my knees. Three other jumpers were jammed in around me. The pilot and the jump master sat in the front of the plane. We were flying in a well-worn Cessna 182, and the straining motor had finally lifted us to the right altitude over the drop zone. I was first in line to jump. At the pilot's signal the jump master opened the door, which pivoted overhead. As he did so, a rush of cold wind slammed into our faces and mixed with the churning roar of the propeller—a nearly deafening crescendo.

"Feet out!" he shouted, and I complied by sticking my feet out the door and placing them firmly on the step over the wheelbase. The wind was whipping my pant legs. I had conditioned myself not to be affected by the sight of the distant ground, which was now more than three thousand feet below. I held my left arm firmly across my chest as I had been instructed, guarding against any accidental hang-ups or snags of the ripcord that controlled the reserve chute. Any incidental opening at this point would spring my chute out into the rushing wind and likely jerk me out of the plane, with tragic results. With my right hand I grasped the wing strut tightly, facing forward against the wind.

"Move out!" was the next command, and I stood up to exit the plane, moving further out onto the wing, working hand over hand on the strut. The wind was blowing in my face and making it difficult to breathe. Soon my feet were free and blown backward, my body horizontal with the ground. Exiting the aircraft should be accomplished smoothly and automatically, and so far everything was going fine.

"Go!" was the next command, but I did not let go. I held on! I looked at the jump master, somewhat surprised at myself for hesitating. He smiled at me and repeated the command.

I let go of the wing and fell into open space. I immediately started to count one thousand one, one thousand two, and at the same time I remembered I was supposed to arch my back. By this time I heard a loud "pop," and the straps of my parachute jerked roughly against my legs and shoulders. The static line had opened my chute, and I gazed up at the beautiful, round, white blossom overhead upon which my life depended. I searched for and quickly found the steering toggles on the cords, first on my left and then on my right.

I could hear the faint hum of the Cessna as it continued on. There was the soft flutter of the parachute silk, but otherwise I was alone in beautiful, all-encompassing silence. The air was cool and sweet. Utah Lake was in view, as well as the beautiful surrounding mountains and valleys. The colorful patchwork quilt below was made up of growing fields and pastures trimmed with threads of dirt roads and fence lines. I could just make out the airstrip in the distance. This beautiful experience was possible because of faith placed in a few silk and nylon threads.

What glorious experiences await us as we put faith in our Heavenly Father and the ties of faith in his omnipotent power! It was the Apostle Paul who counseled us "that [our] faith should not stand in the wisdom of men, but in the power of God" (1 Corinthians 2:5).

Sometimes in life it is very difficult to "let go," but the exercise of true faith usually requires us to "let go" of something. Faith—that is, faith in the Lord Jesus Christ—is so fundamental that it is called the first principle of the gospel.

To let go of the airplane strut and free-fall into open space meant commitment—total commitment. Once I had let go, there was no looking back for help, no changing my mind, no half-hearted trial nor tentative exploring. In similar fashion the Savior cautioned his followers: "No man, having put his hand to the plough, and looking back, is fit for the kingdom of God" (Luke 9:62).

True faith means "letting go." Young men and women accepting mission calls or Church service calls should do so with complete confidence that they may put themselves in the Lord's hands and he will look out for them. Those who accept with timid heart and question as they enter the service of the Lord are similar to one hanging on to the strut of an airplane wing.

Total commitment is also required in marriage. One entering into this sacred bond should do so without looking back. To do otherwise is to forfeit much of what is required to make such a union everlasting. To "look back" or to enter with timid heart is to withhold total devotion and thus to weaken the bond that requires all-out effort to succeed.

Our fears can weaken our faith if we permit, just as looking down at the ground from an altitude of three thousand feet might intimidate a parachutist. On one occasion the Apostle Peter had such great faith that he actually walked on the water, "but when he saw the wind boisterous, he was afraid; and beginning to sink, he cried, saying, Lord, save me" (Matthew 14:30). Then, relying on the Savior's faith, he safely reached the boat and temporal safety.

Sometimes we subject ourselves to unnecessary trauma in making decisions simply because our commitment is not great enough. The person truly committed to the gospel does not have to decide whether to give in to temptations: He is not tempted to smoke or drink or use harmful drugs. The question of moral conduct is not a serious question for him because he has already decided on his course of action when he makes the commitment to live the gospel fully. Without this commitment he is out of control, influenced by fad and fashion, peers and persuasion.

That which we do, let us do with faith, nothing wavering, "for he that wavereth is like a wave of the sea driven with the wind and tossed" (James 1:6).

Those who place their faith and trust in God and who "make the jump" are promised that "eye hath not seen, nor ear heard, neither have entered into the heart of man, the things which God hath prepared for them that love him" (1 Corinthians 2:9).

3

True or False

For a while in my seminary class, I had been stressing the need for honesty, explaining to my students that many times we don't even know our integrity is being tested. I had shared with them experiences like Mr. Larkin's at the corner drugstore. He had told me that Alfred could not be trusted.

"How do you know?" I inquired.

"Well," he said, "often when I have lots of customers and I'm the only salesperson in the store, I let young people make their own change from the cash drawer. Recently, I started coming up short, so I carefully counted out the cash before and after several youngsters had made their own change. They were all honest with me except Alfred. I gave him two chances, and he failed me both times. So now I know that Alfred can't be trusted."

Taken from "True . . . or . . . False," Wayne B. Lynn (*New Era,* September 1978). Copyright © 1978 The Church of Jesus Christ of Latter-day Saints. Used by permission.

"Have you told him?" I asked.

"No, I never have. I just watch him very closely. I hope he never asks me for a job or for a recommendation."

So my class should have been prepared for the snap quiz I gave them that Thursday afternoon. There were twenty questions, a true-or-false test covering material we had discussed during the week. They finished the test just as the bell rang for dismissal.

"Please pass your papers to the center of the aisle," I instructed.

Later that evening I very carefully graded each paper, recording the score in my grade book but leaving no marks on the papers.

When the class assembled the next morning, I passed the papers back and, as usual, asked that each student grade his own paper.

I read each question aloud and with a word of explanation announced the correct answer. Every answer was accompanied by the usual student groan or sigh of relief at having given a wrong or right response.

"Please count five off for each one missed and subtract the total from one hundred," I instructed.

"Your scores please. John?"

"85."

"Susan?"

"95."

"Harold?"

"80."

"Arnold?"

"90."

"Mary?"

The response could hardly be heard: "45."

I went on, putting the grades in my grade book, carefully recording each oral report next to the grade I had recorded the night before. The comparison was revealing.

A stillness settled on the class when I explained what I had done. Many did not look up from their desks; others exchanged furtive glances or quick smiles.

I spoke quietly to my students.

"Some of you may wish to talk to me privately about our experience here today. I would like that.

"This was a different kind of test. This was a test for honesty. Were you true or false? I noticed that many of you looked at Mary when she announced her score of 45. Mary, if you don't mind, would you please stand up? I want each of you to know that in my book Mary just achieved the highest score in class. You make me feel very proud, Mary."

Mary looked up rather timidly at first, then her eyes glistened as she broke into a smile and rose to her feet. I had never seen Mary stand so tall.

4

The Day Our School Burned Down

We were lined up along the edge of the sidewalk next to the curb as straight as a flock of crows on a barbed-wire fence.

We had been told by reliable sources that a more boisterous bunch had never graced the halls of our elementary school. Today, however, we were on our best behavior as a requirement for witnessing a great display of skill. Even the mayor was there wearing his dark suit and white shirt, his collar button straining to hold everything together. Somehow, Mayor Smith still looked like a mechanic even when he left his garage and shed his coveralls.

But our attention was not on the mayor. It was focused on our school principal, Mr. Redding, and the event that was about to take place. Mr. Redding was standing next to some of the teachers at the street corner, his right hand aloft, firmly grasping a stopwatch that was held up for all to see.

This was a great day! Not only were we released from our classroom prisons, but we were to witness the unparalleled skills of the volunteer fire department!

Already we could hear the siren wailing and bells clanging. We strained on tiptoe to be the first to see the fire truck coming. A cheer erupted from one hundred boys and girls as the bright red truck came into sight.

It rounded the corner on squealing tires, with dust flying and dogs barking. Three brightly clad firemen jumped from the moving truck and braced their feet against the ground, holding firmly to the long, limp canvas hose. The spool whirled as the hose unwound and the moving truck pulled over to stop near the closest fire hydrant.

I yelled "Hi" to Bill Jenkins, but he had no time to talk to kids. He was a member of the volunteers, drilled and trained to a fine edge of efficiency. There was an economy in every movement.

Precious seconds were ticking off the stopwatch, but already the hose was trained on the imaginary flames licking at the walls of our house of learning.

The hose was quickly coupled to the hydrant and the nozzle trained upon our hypothetical blaze. A volunteer ran to the hydrant with a special wrench to turn it on. A look of alarm came upon his face—the wrench didn't fit.

There was a scurry as the truck was ransacked to find the crucial missing wrench.

The search continued, and the watch kept ticking.

Buzzy Harris was getting nervous. He stood first on one foot and then another. The length of time a boy can stand in line on the edge of a sidewalk has some definite limitations. Buzzy bent over, picked up a small stick, and with a practiced swing inscribed a perfect circle in the soft dirt beside the walk. Into this circle he threw down his best cat's-eye marble. It was an unspoken challenge to anyone willing to take him on in a game of "migs." I was out of the running because Buzz had already taught me how to play. All of my hard-earned marbles were resting securely in his swollen marble bag.

Three boys soon joined him kneeling in the dirt, doing their best to win that cat's-eye and teach Buzz a lesson he'd never forget. Walter was chasing Suzie Adams, trying to pull her hair. She was screaming at the top of her lungs but not really running as fast as she might.

Mr. Redding was becoming visibly agitated. He glanced at the stopwatch still held partially aloft in his tiring right hand. He lowered his arm to rewind the watch.

Meanwhile, our volunteer fire department was searching for the right wrench. A pickup truck had taken off in a wild dash, its tires throwing gravel. It was headed back toward the fire station on a search mission.

Walter had caught Suzie, but what do you do with a cornered wildcat? Three of Suzie's girlfriends had come to her rescue, and there was some question as to whether he would escape alive.

Buzzy was looking for more takers as he poked newly acquired marbles into his bag. Mr. Redding wound his stopwatch. Three boys had come to Walter's rescue, but Suzie was now receiving reinforcements.

There was no longer a straight line. The crows had hopped off the fence.

I glanced at the schoolhouse and our hypothetical fire. I decided that by now the fire would have consumed the bottom floor, engulfed the second floor, and spread to the principal's office on the third.

Meanwhile, our volunteer fire department was still looking for the right wrench. The watch kept ticking.

No one really noticed when the pickup truck came

screeching back on the scene. Mr. Redding and the other teachers were busy picking boys and girls off a "dog pile." Walter and Suzie were on the bottom and getting squashed. Buzzy was being threatened by a larger opponent who said he was only playing "funs," not "keeps," and wanted his marbles back. Mayor Smith had quietly gone back to his garage.

Suddenly, the long white hose that had lain limp and useless began to take on life. The swelling motion began moving along its length toward the nozzle. Our volunteer firemen were sitting in the shade of the tree with the nozzle lying inertly in their laps. Suddenly the hose came to life. Like an angry cobra, it raised itself posed to strike, lashing out in every direction. Our volunteers bravely tried to control the maverick stream, but it kept dodging from their grasp. Dirt and grass were being washed down to native gravel, and mud was flying everywhere.

Our firemen didn't catch the runaway hose. It caught them. But they grabbed it and held on. It took three of them to control it, and, in the process, Mr. Redding was drenched, along with the rest of the faculty. The few crows still on the fence were unceremoniously washed off. Eventually, the stream was pointed in the right direction toward the imagined embers that had once been our schoolhouse. Mr. Redding promptly said, "All right, that's it! Let's go back inside!" It was Johnny Trump who asked the obvious question, "How long did it take, Mr. Redding? How long did it take?" There was no response.

The question was now chorused by a multitude, "How long did it take, Mr. Redding?" With some difficulty, Mr. Redding extracted his run-down stopwatch from a wet pocket. With a sigh of resignation he said, "Twenty-nine minutes, fourteen and five-tenths seconds."

I glanced over at our hypothetical fire. Our schoolhouse had just burned down.

Through the years I have observed again and again that bright uniforms and shiny engines are useless if we don't have the right wrench. Success comes to those who plan ahead and pay attention to details. Since that day on the school ground I have never accepted a responsibility without asking myself, "Am I really prepared? Do I have the right wrench?"

5

Skin Your Own Skunks

She was an attractive young girl, self-conscious and sweet, a tenth-grade student enrolled in my high school seminary class. "Excuse me, can I please talk to you in your office, alone?"

"Certainly, why don't you come in? We still have a few minutes before class starts. Now, what can I do for you?"

"Well, my brother"—she wrinkled up her nose, took on a look of patient tolerance, and started over again, "my brother thinks he's a trapper. He traps all kinds of animals. This morning when he checked his traps before going to school, he found that he had caught a skunk! It wasn't dead, either. When he came home mother ran him out of the house. She made him undress outside and come into the house with only a towel wrapped around him to take a bath. Our whole place is smelled up!"

I laughed and asked, "Well, June, how can I help you?"

She smiled at me through watery eyes on the verge of

tears. "Please just give me an honest answer. All the kids on the bus and here at school are teasing me and saying that I smell like a skunk. Will you please just tell me—do I?"

The situation was more humorous to me, I'm sure, than it was to June. I wanted to help her smile through her tears.

"Let's put it this way, June," I said gently. "If we are going to continue this conversation, I will need to open my office door and a couple of windows."

"Really?"

"Really."

"May I use your telephone to call home?"

"You may, and while you're doing that I think I will open a window."

Later, I purchased a little glass figurine of a mother skunk, which I glued to a piece of petrified wood. I then glued felt to the bottom of the wood to keep it from scratching furniture and gave it to June as a Christmas present.

Remembering this incident, I have pondered upon how often innocent people are victims of others' folly. A negative association sometimes hurts the innocent more than the offender himself. But more important, and while I'm speaking of skunks, I would like to address the subject of "skinning your own skunks." I have frequently used this phrase in connection with performing an unpleasant task. Have you ever noticed how we seem to find time to do the pleasant things first? It is easy to avoid, postpone, or even delegate distasteful chores that are rightfully ours. One gauge of manhood and personal self-mastery might be our success in disciplining ourselves to do those things that are rightfully our responsibility, as distasteful as they may be. It is morally wrong to shift responsibility because of fear or the unpleasant nature of a responsibility. As easy as it may seem to find ways to circumvent, postpone, or otherwise avoid responsibility, the truth is that every man should learn to "skin his own skunks."

To illustrate, let me tell you about an experience I had shortly after I graduated from college. I found it necessary to borrow some money from the local bank. When the note came due I was still having financial challenges. The bank sent me several reminders but I did not respond; I hadn't decided how to handle the unpleasant task of clearing up my overdue debt. Bank officials soon notified my father since it was upon his good reputation that the loan was granted to me.

My father asked me about it when I stopped by his home and suggested that we go to the bank together to straighten it out. I was fully expecting him to pay the bill and extend our apologies for the late payment, but this was not his intention at all. Instead, he had me meet with the loan officer and work out an extended schedule of monthly time payments until the debt was retired.

That was a valuable lesson to me in several ways. Not only did I learn to communicate my problems to others and work out solutions, but I also learned that I was expected to "skin my own skunks."

6

Our Own Track

Not long ago, I visited an elaborate recording studio in Hollywood, California. The isolation booths were of particular interest to me.

Standing in the booth, one can hear, observe, and participate with everything going on in the main recording room, yet his voice or the musical instrument he might be playing can be recorded separately and distinctly from any other sounds. Most recording tapes now used, we are told, are multiple track. Each track on the tape provides for a separate recording, thus permitting many combinations of sound in the finished recording.

"Do you mean that while I am standing in this isolation booth, a band can be playing right next to me, yet my voice alone will be recorded?" I asked the operator.

"That's exactly right," was his reply. "When we were recording a lot of hard rock groups," he continued, "the total group really had an effect on each member. The singer would stand here in this booth and really get turned on by the others."

"But his voice was recorded separately?" I inquired.

"Yes," he answered. "When it is played back on the single track, we hear only the voice of the singer."

I have reflected upon this experience from time to time, and the thought has occurred to me that the world in which we live is not so different from this studio. In this life we are each recording on our own single track. We live in a world of discordant voices, each attempting to lure us in a different direction. An orchestration of good and evil sounds surrounds us, and lest we beware, we may be caught up in the spirit of what others are doing and react accordingly. Our actions may be influenced by the glamour and fads of our day, but our performance is recorded on a single track.

For example, the youth who harms himself with drugs in response to the influence of friends will pay personally in the privacy of his own soul. The number of others who might be caught in the same trap is then of small importance to the individual.

Mobs may gather and in a spirit of mobocracy they may commit acts contrary to the law; but when an accounting is called for by an earthly tribunal, each man must stand alone. We have reason to suppose that our heavenly tribunal will not be so different. The Lord has told us, "So then every one of us shall give account of himself to God" (Romans 14:12).

Perhaps the Lord has his "isolation booths" where the things we do or say are being recorded. The Lord has said: "But I say unto you, that every idle word that men shall speak, they shall give account thereof in the day of judgment. For by thy words thou shalt be justified, and by thy words thou shalt be condemned." (Matthew 12:36–37.)

The prophet Mormon told us: "Ye must all stand before the judgment-seat of Christ, yea, every soul who belongs to the whole human family of Adam; and ye must stand to be judged of your works, whether they be good or evil" (Mormon 3:20).

We will, in this life, be surrounded by many voices both good and evil; but God in his infinite wisdom has given us our agency to choose which voices we will follow. Each must choose his own path.

7

A Still Small Voice

Only a fool or a fisherman would be up at this early hour, and as I reflected upon it, I wasn't sure there was a great deal of difference between the two.

It was 3:00 A.M. on a cold winter morning. The month was February, and the place was northern Wyoming, where I was teaching school in a lovely little town called Byron. Not too far west from where we lived was the Shoshone Reservoir, more commonly called the Buffalo Bill Dam. It was located near Cody, Wyoming, next to the highway leading toward the east entrance to Yellowstone Park. This was great fishing country, and a little cold weather didn't bother us natives at all. Reports of other successes were sufficient to get us out of our warm beds on this cold Saturday morning. My father arrived at my home and put our lunches and fishing gear into my car while I scraped frost off the windshield. The stars were winking brightly and the cold air was sweet and crisp. Before leaving the house we paused for a moment and kneeled together in prayer to ask for the Lord's protection and for his Spirit to guide us through the day. Two more stops and we would be on our way. Our first stop was for my friend Rick. When our lights beamed into his driveway he was alerted to our arrival. Dressed like an Eskimo, he appeared immediately at the door with a large iron bar in hand that I had recently transformed into an ice pick for him. A hearty greeting, a loading of gear, and then on to our last stop at a small stream of water flowing from a natural spring nearby. This was where we kept our live minnows.

The car soon warmed up as we began our fifty-mile journey to the lake. We loosened our heavy clothing, not wanting to get too warm. The conversation was animated even at this early hour as thoughts of the big ones filled our imaginations. Mackinaw, rainbows, and browns were all biting, and winter trout is as delicious as anything you can name.

We were racing daybreak because early hours seemed to be the best time to fish.

Two rivers flow into the huge lake we were headed for: the North Fork of the Shoshone River and the South Fork. Fish often gather where the rivers flow into the lake. They lie in wait facing upstream as their food supply floats down the current from the river.

We decided on fishing the South Fork side of the lake, so we took the left turn at the highway junction a few miles west of Cody. It was still dark when we parked the car and bundled up for our foray out upon the frozen surface. The lake shone like a huge sparkling jewel in the moonlight. Loaded with gear, we wended our way down the slope for nearly a hundred yards to reach the sandy beach and edge of the lake. Pieces of driftwood and melted snowbanks marked the crooked shoreline. We took our first steps upon the slippery surface with some trepidation as we cautiously moved out on the ice.

As we took those first few steps, a strong feeling of apprehension flooded over me, and I noted that my father had a similar impression.

"Let's just fish right here," my father suggested.

"No way, they're biting out where the river feeds in," was Rick's rebuttal. "We'll never catch anything here."

"This ice scares me," Dad said. "Somehow I don't trust it. Let's just give it a try here near the shore."

"Here, let me show you," Rick countered, and he began chipping into the icy surface with his sharp new ice pick. In a moment he had chopped a hole over fifteen inches deep and was still going strong. "This would hold up a truck" was his comment, and he was right. But our destination was about one-half mile out on the ice, and that's a long, risky way to go from shore. We disregarded our apprehensions and moved out onto the lake, but the nagging feeling persisted—not one of logic but just a gut-level feeling that we "hadn't oughta."

We were among the first to arrive at our predetermined spot. We were not alone, but the lake was so huge that the parties were widely separated in relative isolation.

Let me explain a few of the technical aspects of this sort of fishing. Most parties carry an old iron bucket filled with ashes and soaked with kerosene. This can be torched and, with an occasional stirring, will burn the entire morning to help keep us warm.

The air was so cold that morning we could hear voices from across the lake as clearly as if the people were standing next to us. The movement of the water underneath the expanding ice caused it to creak and crack and give off constant groanings and rifle-like retorts.

We had trudged across the vast ice and found our way up near the south confluence, having crossed over the lake from the east side. Now, with our fire lit for warmth, we proceeded to dig several fishing holes. The heavy rod we used for an ice pick was made from an old car axle to which I had welded a piece of leaf spring. This spring was cut to form three long teeth, each sharpened to a point. Ice would really fly and a hole in the eighteen-inch thick ice could be carved out in a few minutes. The round holes we chopped were about eighteen to twenty inches in diameter. As we chopped, we scooped out the ice chips, being careful not to penetrate through to the water until the hole was nearly complete.

Once the hole was chopped we rigged our poles. Fish-and-game laws require the use of a fish pole, but we actually land the fish by raising the line hand over hand. Fish poles are useless here because the eyelets soon freeze solid.

We fastened a large hook to several feet of leader that was tied to the line. About eighteen inches above the hook we placed a relatively heavy bell sinker, heavy enough to carry hook and bait to the bottom. Next, we pushed the hook through the back of a live minnow for bait and lowered him and the weight into the cold, green water. We let out the line hand over hand until we felt the weight strike bottom; then we lifted the line about two feet off the lake bottom and fastened a brightly colored red-and-white bobber to the line at water level. We were allowed only one line each, but we helped watch each other's lines.

When the bobber started sinking or bobbing up and down, our hearts would go up and down with it! We knew what was on the other end! A skillful pause as the bobber sank, then a quick jerk on the line to set the hook—and the fun started! The beautiful trout we pulled splashing and twisting to the surface weighed one or two pounds each.

Landing a fish every few minutes, we soon found ourselves totally absorbed in this fantastic sport. One huge German brown trout gave us a real run for our money. When he was finally landed we estimated his weight as four pounds. Rick had landed him and in his exuberance yelled, "Oh, shucks, he's just a brown. Let's kick him back in!" As he spoke he gave a fake kick toward the fish and the hole in the ice. The fish chose that very moment to leap in the air, and before Rick could pull back his foot, he had kicked him directly back into the hole. Mr. Brown promptly made a life-saving exit into the deep waters. All was quiet for a minute and then we broke into laughter. It was the biggest fish we had caught all day, and we had kicked him back down the hole! It was too funny for words.

Things quieted down a little after that as we continued fishing. By this time, the sun had risen and was shining brightly. We had even shed our heavy coats. We had recently had a few nice days like this when the weather suddenly turned unseasonably warm.

My attention was turned toward my father, who was in the process of catching a fish, when an overpowering sense of urgency flooded through my body. Looking over at my father I spoke with a feeling of near alarm: "Dad, I think we need to get out of here right now." Without argument my dad replied, "I think so too; let's do it." To my amazement, he pulled his line away from a sure catch and began gathering up his gear. Rick looked at us strangely but didn't argue. We nearly had our limit anyway.

With a heavy string of fish in one hand and my fish pole and gear box in the other, I led our trio in the trek back over the lake. Our sense of urgency persisted, so I walked quickly. With my attention focused ahead I was totally surprised when, without warning, the ice under my feet gave way, and I found myself immersed in icy waters to my armpits. My outthrown arms kept me from submerging further. I gave a loud cry in reaction to the cold and the surprise, and as quickly as I could I managed to lift myself out of the hole and onto firmer footing. Quick observation revealed that the ice had formed into small, narrow crystals in a honeycomb pattern. Even though the ice was thick, it would not support my weight but allowed my feet to push through into the frigid water.

Getting back to my feet, I ventured forward again more cautiously. I had traveled perhaps twenty yards when I fell through again. Again I climbed out, and as I did, the shore seemed a mighty long distance away. In reality it was nearly half a mile. Again we ventured forward, and this time when I fell through it became more serious. As I tried to extricate myself, the ice broke off and refused to support my weight. The hole became larger and larger; it was as big as an automobile before I finally found ice strong enough to allow me to climb out.

It was decided that perhaps my father should lead out since he didn't weigh as much as I did. As serious as things looked, we all laughed when he fell through. He gave a loud, "Hooo! this water's cold!" Rick was next to lead us, being the smallest of the three; however, he soon fell through and, like me, could not find ice to support himself. I noted with alarm that he was beginning to panic, and he had a wild, glazed look in his eyes. As carefully as I could, I crawled over to him on my stomach and extended a helping hand. Our fingers finally touched, and I dragged him nearly exhausted out upon the ice. When he recovered slightly, he rose to his feet and started almost running toward shore. He succeeded in going nearly one hundred yards without incident. Pausing briefly, he turned back toward us and yelled, "If you make it out to here I think you'll be all right!" Having said this, he turned, took a few steps, and promptly fell through the ice.

Our return was a nightmare. We soon realized that if we had tarried even a few minutes longer, we would have had a cold watery grave. As it turned out, we struggled closer and closer to the distant shore. As we walked, we searched for the right-colored ice or stronger snowpack, but it was totally unpredictable. We never knew when we would suddenly sink into the frigid waters of the lake.

We shouted warnings to other fishermen who were closer to shore. They saw our predicament and scampered to safety. In a true act of cowardice and lack of consideration, they packed their gear and left, leaving us in our circumstances although our warning shouts had literally saved them.

I can't say we were truly frightened until we drew within about 100 yards from shore. By now, we had fallen in numerous times but had persistently pressed forward. With each step we took, the surface of the ice would ripple like a blanket many yards ahead. It looked as though the entire ice cap was about to disintegrate. Both the ice and the temperature would have made swimming to safety impossible.

At last Rick somehow reached the shore and managed to build a fire from driftwood. A game warden had parked his truck by my car and had joined Rick. They were both intently watching our progress.

It is hard to describe our feelings when our feet finally touched the solid shore at almost the same instant. We looked back over our tortuous path marked by holes and water. Without question even a few minutes delay in leaving our first position would have meant certain tragedy. We were distracted for a moment from our reverie by an insensitive game warden who seemed more concerned with seeing our fishing licenses than enquiring about our physical well-being. As we warmed ourselves around the fire, our thoughts returned to those early morning hours when we first stepped out upon the ice and to the warning "feeling" that we had both disregarded. This had all happened only a few hours before, but it seemed like ages ago. Although we had failed to heed the Lord's warning, he had given us another chance and had warned us again. This time we had listened. I recalled as I turned to warm myself in front of the fire how we had knelt at home that morning and asked the

Lord for guidance. Yet we had disregarded the guidance when it was given. My thoughts turned to Nephi of old as he scolded his older brothers: "He hath spoken unto you in a still small voice, but ye were past feeling, that ye could not feel his words" (1 Nephi 17:45).

The Lord had almost shouted in our ears, and we listened and were saved. We joshed each other on the way home; it was a way of relieving tension. Rick said little. He was embarrassed at his own behavior.

I was complimented on how fresh I had kept the fish. I had held them tightly in my hand and only after we reached safety ashore had I become consciously aware of them once again.

I had dunked them frequently in cold water. Unfortunately, I was dunked along with them. That night I knelt on the same livingroom carpet. This time my prayer was one of sincere thanksgiving. It was also a prayer of resolve that I would try to live so as to merit the promptings of "that still small voice" and to be prepared to hear and feel it when it came. I prayed for faith and courage to act upon those divine impressions.

The fish were delicious, and you might also safely say that it was a fishing trip we would not soon forget.

II. Overcoming Obstacles

8

Young Courage

Sometimes, we can gain the courage or determination to succeed through the example of others. This is especially true when we see those who have handicaps or who are under difficult circumstances rise above them and succeed.

The story of Don Smith has helped me to appreciate my blessings of health and my opportunities more fully and may help to inspire others.

Don was a young man when I first met him.

The youth I saw confined to a wheelchair was a startling contrast to the boy I remembered from the year before. I remembered him as a happy, eighteen-year-old Indian boy whose swift, strong legs had carried him up and down the basketball courts. But that was yesteryear. This day he was in a wheelchair, and his dark eye and handsome smile

Taken from the *Improvement Era*, Wayne B. Lynn, May 1978. Copyright © 1978 The Church of Jesus Christ of Latter-day Saints. Used by permission.

caused me to stand in awe of his youthful courage.

I had first met Don a couple of years before and learned that he was a convert to the Church. His widowed mother lived in a remote section of the Navajo Indian reservation, and he was a participant in the Indian student placement program. His school work was excellent; he played the piano skillfully; and with the same slim, brown fingers he could paint beautiful pictures or strum the guitar in accompaniment to his clear, soft voice. Don's personality was pleasant, his standards high, and his testimony strong. He was soon to graduate from high school, and his plans were to spend a short time with his people on the reservation before returning to live with his foster parents, where he would work in preparation for his expected call to the mission field.

Life seems to have a way of changing the most carefully made plans, but no one would have expected the traumatic experience that awaited Don. His fun on the reservation was cut short by painful events, and his mission began in a much different way than one would have imagined.

While riding in the back of a pickup with some of his friends, Don accidentally fell out onto the hard, black pavement and skidded painfully along its rough surface. That was the last thing he remembered until he awoke in a hospital bed, his body in physical torment.

An excruciating pain in his back persisted through the long night, and as the new day began, Don found himself unable to move his arms, hands, or legs. He was paralyzed from his neck down!

Following an emergency operation, he awoke in a recovery room with the pain in his mended back subsiding; but he was also painfully aware of his helpless limbs that refused to respond to his efforts to move them.

Don's concerned doctors had little hope that his condition would ever change. As he lay helpless in his hospital bed, fighting back the tears of discouragement, he poured

out the feelings of his heart to his Heavenly Father, asking
for strength to endure and for a recovery from his affliction
if it were his will.

Night after night while others slept, Don struggled
through the long, dark hours attempting to move the helpless hands that lay inert by his side. He would pray and try,
pray and try, repeating over and over in his mind, "I can do
it, I can do it, I can do it!" Then, as the early morning light
filtered softly through the blinds of his window, he would
surrender himself wearily to a merciful sleep.

On one such interminable night, Don's heart suddenly
pounded with excitement as he felt an almost impercepti-
ble movement in one of his fingers! Holding his breath in
suspense, he moved his finger again!

There was no sleep for Don that night. A wonderful,
elated feeling of hope buoyed his troubled spirit and gave
him renewed determination to regain the use of his hands.

Each night became a new adventure as, gradually, with
great effort and perseverance, the use of his hands and arms
slowly returned to him.

In the meantime Don's doctor had procrastinated the
unwelcome task of informing him that he must mentally
prepare himself to accept his paralysis as an unalterable fact
of his young life.

With great difficulty the doctor broke this news to Don.
It was a poignant moment for the good doctor, who turned
quickly away to conceal his emotion. As he made his exit,
he stole a last glance at Don lying quietly in his bed. Just at
this moment, Don reached his arm up to the head rail of his
bed and pulled himself into a more comfortable position.
The startled doctor could not contain himself. "Do that again,
Don! Do that again!" he shouted with excitement. Soon the
room was swarming with nurses and doctors who came running to learn the cause of the great commotion. It was a
moment to be remembered.

Although Don was happy to feel the strength gradually return to his arms and hands, he had to fight back the tears when he looked down at his helpless legs.

In these trying circumstances he began to fulfill his desire to be a missionary. He told his roommate about the Book of Mormon and gave him a copy to read. Charles, a Hopi Indian boy, immediately became engrossed in the book, and, when darkness came at the close of the day, he continued reading. He devoured the words of this book for three days and two nights, jealous of the time it took to eat or rest. Finally, when he had turned the last page, he rose from his bed and walked over near Don's side and asked, "Don, where did you get this book? I have shared in the traditions of my people that we hold to be sacred. Many of our traditions are written in this book. Where did you get it?"

Don happily shared his testimony with this new friend as he told him of the restoration of the gospel and of its special meaning to them as Lamanites, a covenant race and descendants of the Book of Mormon people.

Soon after this Charles was released to go home, anxious to share this new message with family and friends. Don was moved to a rehabilitation center in Denver, Colorado. He was quite unprepared for what he encountered at his new residence in the paralytic ward. Everyone seemed depressed, discouraged, and despondent. Patients could not understand how Don, who was in an equally distressing condition, could seem so happy. Some of them asked, "Why are you always so happy and smiling?" Don replied, "My smile keeps the tears from my eyes, and my laughter keeps the lump from my throat."

With courageous determination Don took advantage of the special care he now received. Long after others would tire and leave the gymnasium, he would remain—trying, trying, trying. Through his valiant effort, accompanied by humble petitions to his Heavenly Father, he was finally strong enough to go up and down the parallel bars alone; then he was able to walk with braces and crutches. His new mobility permitted him to attend Church services. This spiritual comfort brought him great joy, but he was totally surprised by the reception he was given upon his return to the hospital. Everyone teased him for going to church! In his characteristic way Don's smile merely broadened at their taunting. He resolved to do something about the gloomy atmosphere in this, his new home, so he happily embarked upon the next chapter of his mission.

In the days that followed, he could be seen wheeling himself down hallways and into every room where patients would receive him, preaching the gospel to all who would listen. He became known good-naturedly as "the prophet," a title that he accepted graciously.

In the evenings he often lifted his voice in song as he accompanied himself with his guitar. Others began to join in, and the spirit spread. Friday nights soon became known as the time for a hootenanny, and patients joined together with voices raised in song and laughter. Patients began to smile and call each other by name. This new spirit extended into other activities as well.

One of the more dramatic examples was the organizing of the wheelchair Olympics.

On the day agreed upon, patients wheeled excitedly from place to place as they marked out a course for the coming events. Wheelchairs were lined up at a starting line, while occupants leaned forward, intently waiting for the starting signal. The signal was given, and they were off in a flurry of wheels and laughter. After a breather and an untangling of wheels, patients were given a chance to challenge other wheelchairs. Don looked around, and pointing his finger at one of the chairs, said, "I challenge that chair."

"Don, you can't do that," the astonished attendant replied. "That chair has a motor!"

The competitive young man was undaunted and remained firm; so a course was set, and an eager audience waited expectantly for the signal to begin this most unusual race. Soon the signal was given and Don's hands fairly flew as he propelled his chair toward the finish line. When he had gained full momentum, he ventured a cautious look toward his opponent, only to discover that he was shifting to a higher gear! To complicate matters further, a woven wire fence was stretched a few short feet behind the finish line.

With the heart of a champion, Don ducked his head and gave it everything he had. He crossed the line only inches ahead of his opponent and crashed happily into the wire fence. He was picked up and dusted off amid excited expressions of admiration. He had won!

All was not happiness for Don, however, for he longed to see his home, his family, and his friends. In spite of his high resolve, his vision clouded when he looked down at his crippled legs. Wonderful Church members tried to fill his hours of need, and Don said, "Through their kindness they put a smile on my face and laughter in my mouth."

As time drew near for him to be released, he began to worry about his acceptance by friends and family upon his return.

The day finally came when his foster parents arrived. It was an ordeal for Don to muster up enough courage to direct the question that had filled his mind completely. "Do you want me to come back?" he asked apprehensively. They softly replied, "Of course, Don. We have a bed waiting for you." The kind response was too much for him! This time his tears flowed freely and mixed with theirs in demonstration of joy and love.

On the night of Don's departure, a special hootenanny was held in his behalf. His many new friends shook the rafters with a song rendered in his honor: "Too Many Chiefs and Not Enough Indians Around This Place."

The courage and spirit of this young man had touched the lives of others and left an indelible impression.

Two of the residing patients and two members of the nursing staff who waved good-bye to Don had embraced the gospel of Jesus Christ as a result of his influence. Many looked to the future with new hope, and each felt a personal loss at his departure.

Upon his return home Don's numerous friends were out to greet him and welcome him back into their circle of friendship. Don soon found a job at an LDS mailbox bookstore that enabled him to meet the payments on his car, a vehicle equipped with special controls that would carry him to his work and to the Mesa Community College where he was enrolled for classes.

As I concluded my visit with him, he handed me a letter. "What is this?" I asked. "It's a letter from my physical therapist in Denver," he smiled in reply.

I unfolded the pages and began to read. "Dear Don," the letter began, "I don't know how to thank you. Yesterday was the happiest day of my life. It was the day I was baptized a member of The Church of Jesus Christ of Latter-day Saints."

I hope I will remember the example of Don. I hope I will remember his parting words when I asked about his future. He looked directly at me and spoke with conviction: "I'll wipe away my tears and let the winds of discouragement blow. I cannot fail, for God is with me."

9

The Winter of Tribulation

Often, we feel we are burdened with more than our share of adversity or discouragement. With this in mind, I would like to share a personal experience with you. My memory is still clear with a sweet experience involving Sister Joyce Jensen, who passed away just a few years ago. I first met her when she was introduced to us—a beautiful, refined lady. She had been approved as one who could assist us with some of the writing of Church lesson materials. Specifically, her assignment was to help with Relief Society lessons. What many people, including myself, didn't know was that Sister Jensen had terminal cancer and that her life expectancy was very short. Her situation was further complicated by a serious heart condition. How easy it would have been for her to retreat from life—to say, "What's the use?" Instead she gracefully and gratefully accepted the call to write. She was given a special priesthood blessing by the director of the department and by her husband, with a promise of mental and physical health to complete this calling.

Almost as if by divine decree, the first lesson she was assigned to write for the sisters of the Church was entitled "The Trial of Your Faith." Perhaps some sisters will remember studying or reading this lesson, little realizing that it was written by someone who spent many hours in bed reading, writing, praying, and applying a very special insight to bless the lives of others. Sister Jensen wrote many letters, completed her entire assignment, and, in her own words, said, "This blessing has literally been fulfilled." She penned some words in reflection that I would like to share with you: "The emotional pressures of living with a terminal illness can be devastating. But I have learned that life can be fully lived one day at a time. Who of us knows when our mission in life will be accomplished and we'll be called home? This morning, as the sun rises, I think of God our Creator, His love for me and His understanding of my struggles. He hears my prayers and knows the secret thoughts of my heart. He knows me entirely and I know something of Him. Because I know He is there and desires my eternal happiness, I can meet this day with joy and faith, no matter what comes. I know there will be days when I will have to call upon all my spiritual strength. But the testing comes one hour and one day at a time."

Sister Jensen penned these verses, which she called "Expectations in Spring."

> Expectations in Spring
>
> I had not thought to see
> The beauty of these blossoms once again
> Nor experience the days of yet another year.
> In the winter of my tribulation
> When life seemed in a balance
> Weighing here and there,
> I thought of other springs

And scarcely hoped to see again
This pink profusion.

If I am here to pick the full ripe fruit
It is because God wills it.
His purposes are His own
And acceptance is an act of faith.
When finally the seasons pass
Without my watching
In some other place I'll know
And hoping, be at peace.

We each have challenges to overcome. What we need amidst the days of our tribulations is to see even more clearly life's purpose and opportunities. I hope that each of us will continue to prepare our lives for service and rich fulfillment. May each of us prepare our fields and plant tender young trees which promise future harvests. May we begin new journeys and move constantly forward, knowing that there will be flowers to smell in pink profusion and mountains to climb and conquer and memories to make and cherish in this arena of todays and tomorrows.

We live in a great day, a day of opportunity with living prophets to counsel and guide us as we continue on our journey. We live in a day of great opportunities with the gospel as a guideline for us—that iron rod which, if we grasp it firmly, will lead us back to the presence of our Heavenly Father after experiencing a life of joy and happiness and fulfillment. May each of us have this beautiful experience in this great adventure called life.

10

Courage to Endure

Only a constant supply of life-giving irrigation water kept the beans, alfalfa, and sugar beets from wilting in the hot July sun; but wet soil and hot weather is "what really makes things grow," and the crops looked good this year.

Days on the farm were long. Most of them started for us in the early light before the sun was up. These were beautiful mornings filled with dew and delicate fragrance, blossoms of clover, newly mown hay, and the damp coolness of the night. Often the stars would be blinking farewell as my father and I perched on the front porch to slip our irrigation boots on. Everyone learned to shake these boots out before putting them on. I remember the morning I forgot. A mouse had taken shelter during the night, and his frantic effort to escape my foot as it filled the boot awakened visions of one of the coiled rattlesnakes that were not uncommon to our area. My boot came off faster than it went on, and the mouse scurried away. I don't know which of us was more startled or relieved.

Changing several streams of water was the way we generally started our day. We would walk to the fields with a shovel over our shoulder and our rubber boots pulled up to keep our pants dry from dew-covered grass.

Moving the water was a process of rapidly changing several canvas dams in the irrigation ditch and shoveling new holes in the ditchbank, damming off the ditches as we went. We would pull the wet, muddy dam from the ditch and race downstream to set it in a new location before the released water could catch up with us. The dam usually managed to brush against us; our Levi's would become crusted with mud until they stiffened, the mud dried, and it crumbled off again.

We were always discovered by hoards of hungry mosquitoes who seemed to know instinctively when our hands would be filled with shovels and dams. They would find a soft spot and drink deeply while we worked. Some of the more fortunate ones would pull stakes and fly off drunkenly with their bloody cargo before our hands were freed. Long-sleeved shirts and a large kerchief under our straw hats were some deterrent, but they were never enough.

When the stream was regulated and each furrow was receiving an equal portion of water, it was time for us to start the livestock chores. We started early because it was never fun to milk cows with the sun on our backs, and the cows needed to be in the pasture while it was still cool and the flies weren't too bad.

With the cows milked, hogs and chickens fed, and the milk separated, it was time to eat breakfast so we could go to work.

On a typical day like this, an incident took place that I still recall. That day my labor continued as we worked in the fields stacking hay. Evening came and the process of changing the water, milking the cows, feeding the pigs and chickens, and separating the milk was repeated. Supper was eaten at 8:00 P.M.

When darkness began its quiet descent, I felt tired but fulfilled. On most nights I would have read a few chapters in a book or listened to the radio before going to bed, but this was Saturday night. A fresh shave, a cool bath, a change of clothes and I felt like a new man.

The popular entertainment and the place to go on Saturday night was the open-air dance held at the dance pavilion. The orchestra seldom got going much before ten o'clock. Thoughts of the live orchestra, pretty girls, and renewed associations swept away any thoughts of being tired.

I drove alone tonight. I had been too busy to ask anyone to go with me. Communication was difficult with no telephones, and, besides, we often went alone and formed groups or paired off at the dance.

The dance was all I expected it to be. Music lifted through the soft evening air and reached me before I could park my car among the many that already encircled the dance pavilion.

The usual type of crowd was standing outside watching, but most were inside dancing. Familiar friends shouted greetings, and I was already glad that I had come. This was one of my first social contacts since returning from the university last spring. No one had changed much. Everyone was dressed in summer dress. The girls seemed prettier than ever.

I joined with a group of acquaintances and was soon caught up in the spirit of their fun. It was good to be among my kind of people.

As we paired off for dancing, I found myself dancing more with Betty than with anyone else. She really looked cute that night. She was soft, quiet, pretty, and very appealing. What was even more exciting—she was obviously glad to see me.

It seemed only natural that we should share a soft drink

and talk together during intermission. While we were talking, one of my friends said, "Hey, Wayne, there's a guy over there wants to see you."

"Who is it?"

"I don't know, but he's over there just outside the gate."

I glanced over and saw him looking toward me and Betty. He was of slender build, several inches taller than I, and my senior by several years. A total stranger to me. I excused myself and weaved my way through the crowd to where he was standing.

"Hey, Buddy," he addressed me. "Come out here; I want to talk to you."

I accommodated him by walking out through the gate, my curiosity aroused but with some apprehension from the unfriendly tone of his voice. Before I could speak he snapped, "What's the idea of dancing with my girl?"

"Who's your girl?"

"Betty."

"Betty? She doesn't act like your girl."

"Come over here and I'll show you whose girl she is," he challenged.

My reply was, "Why should I do that? I'm doing all right as it is."

He was belligerent. "I'm one tough son from Texas, and I'm going to clean your plow."

He was determined, and nothing could dissuade him from trying to "clean my plow."

We walked across the oiled highway near the pavilion and into a barrow pit that was out of sight and sound of most of the crowd. "What have I got myself into?" I asked myself. I saw no way out short of having it out with him or showing pure cowardice.

"Whoever wins the fight can dance with Betty," he said as he flexed his arms and raised his clenched fists in front of him.

He was dressed in tan gabardine pants and a white shirt. I had on a yellow sports shirt which I removed and, placing my glasses in the shirt pocket, draped over a fence post. Underneath I was wearing a white tee shirt. This fellow was determined. He was anxious and he was waiting for me. Inside I was trembling. I approached him and assumed a stance familiar to me from previous boxing experience. I circled him cautiously, manuevering to higher ground until I became his equal in height. His right arm was cocked way back ready to send a blow intended to separate my head from my shoulders. Seeing this, I stepped quickly toward him. He instinctively let fly with his haymaker. I was so close to him that he merely wrapped his arm around me. As we separated, I led with my right, mostly measuring him for distance; but I caught him squarely in the mouth, and his head bobbed back in painful surprise. I was left handed and this often caught my opponents off guard. He was wary now. I threw a couple more right leads his way and tagged him again on the side of his face. With a roar he lowered his head and came at me with both arms flailing. With his head down he couldn't really see where he was going. I side-stepped him easily and brought an uppercut hard into his turned-down face. He was bleeding profusely now from both nostrils, his white shirt spattered with red. I measured him again for a convincing blow, but he had lowered his hands, the fight gone out of him.

"I've had enough," he said. "I thought I was a tough son from Texas, but I'm a tame son from Texas."

I left him standing there. He had managed to smear my arms and tee shirt with blood, so I walked over to a nearby irrigation ditch running full of water. I took off the blood-stained shirt and rinsed my arms and face. I picked up my yellow sports shirt from the fence post and put it and my glasses back on, threw the soiled tee-shirt into the trunk of my car, and went back into the dance. All this had taken place in a few minutes. No one had even missed me.

I mixed in again with the group, taking up where I had left off. Betty looked at me inquiringly, but I didn't say anything and she didn't ask.

Later, I heard a commotion outside the pavilion. A large crowd had gathered around my opponent, and they were all looking in my direction. He was pointing at me. He looked a mess, with blood on his white shirt and tan pants. He looked worse, I am sure, than he really was. The crowd looked at me, clean and neat without a mark on me, then back at him—he looked like he'd been hit with a truck.

The simplest thing to do seemed to be to slip away. I was opening the door of the car when Betty appeared beside me. I motioned her into the car and began driving. It seemed appropriate to ask her for a date to the next dance. I somehow felt I had earned the right.

The crowd was still watching us as we drove away. Needless to say, my reputation was enhanced with this little encounter. I took Betty home with a promised date for the next dance. It was time for me to get home. Tomorrow morning I had to change the water.

This singular experience did not substantially contribute to my humility nor was it really compatible with the gospel as I understood it. In spite of this, if I were being truly honest, I would have to admit that I took some pride in this venture. I rationalized that this was a courageous response to an unpleasant situation.

However, years later while I was serving as a mission president, a much higher level of courage and true Christian charity was demonstrated to me.

Two Elders serving in a remote area were accosted by some rowdies who had been drinking. They first attacked the Elders verbally and then physically. The irony was that the Elders were of sufficient size and skill to have very successfully defended themselves, but they chose not to. The ruffians soon tired of their behavior and left, not without inflicting marks of their physical abuse upon the Elders.

In the days that followed, people learned of what had happened, and their sympathies were with these brave young Elders. Doors opened to them that were previously closed. Several of the young men who had attacked them sought them out one by one and asked forgiveness. A bond of friendship resulted and the Lord's work moved forward.

There are perhaps times when one must resort to physical force, but the highest order of courage is to be able to endure, especially when it is within our power to do otherwise.

11

A Different Kind of Courage

There are many ways for young people to show courage. Sometimes something very dramatic may happen right before us that shows true grit.

Some folks say that the day of heroes has passed. Some people say that the youth of today do not have the courage young people used to have, but I once saw courage displayed that shone so brightly it caused my heart to beat faster and my throat to tighten. I felt like rising to my feet and shouting, "Hurrah! Hurrah!"

It was not in the roaring flames of a burning building where this courage was shown, nor was it a plunge into the icy floodwaters of a roaring river. It was not a reckless dash in front of a speeding auto to save the toddling child, nor was it a display of physical courage to thwart the threatening bully.

It happened instead in a rather common place, for that seems to be where most heroic deeds happen. It happened in a stake priesthood meeting on a hot July afternoon. The chapel was filled to overflowing, and the partition doors leading into the cultural hall had been opened to accommodate the large body of the priesthood. A special spirit seemed to be with us that day as our beloved stake president presided over us and conducted the affairs of the stake.

One lad who appeared to be about the age of a priest sat in a rather conspicuous place on the stand near the stake presidency. I had correctly guessed that he was to take part on the program, and I sympathized with his contained nervousness.

Soon the president announced the young man as the next speaker. He arose quietly and walked the short distance to the stand. His outward composure was calm, but my vantage point near the front of the room permitted me a view of the quivering hands that told of the fear to be conquered.

Taking a deep breath, he began to speak. It was quickly obvious that he had spent much time in preparation. An occasional glance at his notes was all that was required. I began to relax a little in my apprehension for him, but then I noticed that his speech was beginning to come faster and faster. Words were coming so fast that they were being repeated unnecessarily. In the middle of his next sentence he began to stammer. This increased his nervousness to the degree that his stammering continued, making him entirely speechless.

A sympathetic silence filled the room. I longed to reassure him or indicate in some way my sympathy and understanding, but, like the others, I waited. I waited for him to surrender and perhaps try again another day.

I could see the youth waging an inward battle as he stood there before us. Then it happened. He squared his shoulders and girded himself to the task, uttering, as nearly as I can recall, these words: "Brethren, I ask for an interest in your faith and prayers that I might have sureness of speech."

It was as if I had seen a miracle. He began again to speak, slowly, deliberately, but with sureness and conviction. His young voice rang out in a message that thrilled my soul. It is not his words I remember, but stamped indelibly upon my memory is the message of the boy himself.

Somehow, I will never feel the same again when I am called upon to perform a difficult task. Perhaps I can take a few steps up the same trail blazed by this brave young man, for he had climbed the mount of moral courage and stood unflinching upon its precipice.

His talk was soon completed. He gathered his notes and turned away from the stand, and for a moment I saw more than a young man in a white shirt. I saw a knight in shining armor with a sword at his side and a token of victory in his hand. The words of a song surged into my consciousness so strongly that they seemed to be crying out to be heard: "Behold! A royal army, with banner, sword, and shield, is marching forth to conquer on life's great battlefield. Its ranks are filled with soldiers, united, bold, and strong, who follow their Commander and sing their joyful song: Victory, victory"! ("Behold! A Royal Army," *Hymns*, no. 251.)

And victory will be the song if the ranks are filled with young men like this.

12

Free to Soar

One windy spring day, I observed young people having fun using the wind to fly their kites. Multicolored creations of varying shapes and sizes filled the skies like beautiful birds darting and dancing in the heady atmosphere above the earth. As the strong winds gusted against the kites, a string kept them in check. Instead of blowing away with the wind, they arose against it to achieve great heights. They shook and pulled, but the restraining string and the cumbersome tail kept them in tow, facing upward and against the wind. As the kites struggled and trembled against the string, they seemed to say, "Let me go! Let me go! I want to be free!" They soared beautifully even as they fought the imposed restriction of the string. Finally, one of the kites succeeded in breaking loose. "Free at last" it seemed to say. "Free to fly with the wind."

Yet freedom from restraint simply put it at the mercy of an unsympathetic breeze. It fluttered ungracefully to the ground and landed in a tangled mass of weeds and string against a dead bush. "Free at last"—free to lie powerless in the dirt, to be blown helplessly along the ground, and to lodge lifeless against the first obstruction.

How much like kites we sometimes are. The Lord gives us adversity and restrictions, rules to follow from which we can grow and gain strength. Restraint is a necessary counterpart to the winds of opposition. Some of us tug at the rules so hard that we never soar to reach the heights we might have obtained. We keep part of the commandment and (pardon the pun) never rise high enough to get our tails off the ground.

Let us each rise to the great heights our Heavenly Father has in store for us, recognizing that some of the restraints that we may chafe under are actually the steadying force that helps us ascend and achieve.

13

To All the World

I was seated at the head table next to a visiting General Authority. The event was a fund-raising effort for the general missionary fund of the Church. The stake had chosen a Polynesian Luau as the way to raise money through voluntary contributions. The hall was beautifully decorated. Several pigs had been barbequed and an air of festivity prevailed. Flower leis flown from Hawaii were draped around our necks and someone was picking away on a Hawaiian steel guitar.

Then something happened so quietly that it went largely unobserved. An older man, dressed in the way ranchers dress when they go to town, approached our table. He was wearing tan gabardine pants, neatly creased, which covered the tops of his cowboy boots and were held in place by a wide leather belt with a silver buckle. His skin was dry, browned and wrinkled by many suns. His days had been spent with the cattle and out in the desert range lands. Held in a calloused hand was a check, which he handed to the General Authority with this question, "Is this going right into the world mission?" After the old rancher was assured that this was the case, he handed over the check. I smiled to myself when I could see to whom the check was made out: "The Missionary Department to All the World, The Church of Jesus Christ of Latter-day Saints." The amount was for $1,000.00! As I returned home from this pleasant event I discussed with my fellow passengers the quiet commitment and example of this humble man. I shared my observation without mentioning any names. "This good brother will return home tonight," I observed. "He will enter the door to his home—it is weather-beaten and old. It requires an extra push to open it. The screen door is sagging and has been patched in several places. He will turn on the light, which will reveal his livingroom couch. It will be covered neatly with a blanket because the cushions are worn and the stuffing is showing through in a place or two. He would buy another one but he can't afford it." Such is the quiet dedication of these humble Saints.

And this is how this humble little Arizona stake quietly and without fanfare raised $58,000 one night for the "Missionary Fund to All the World," and in so doing moved our Heavenly Father's work forward and consecrated their lives through simple sacrifice. Upon such firm foundations the kingdom of God moves forward quietly, strongly to its divine destiny.

III. Working with Others

14

The Least Among Us

Our small, rented Volkswagen had carried us deep into the interior of central Mexico. We bumped along on this fascinating journey over winding dirt roads through small villages and past clusters of farm homes. Now, as it grew dark, the homes could be seen only by their flickering lights. It was Sunday night and the hour was growing late. The heat of the afternoon lingered in the quiet summer air. We trusted our friend, who was driving and who had lived here before, to find the Church members' home. We had asked him to help us get to know some of the members and to learn more about the country.

A cloud of dust followed us when we finally pulled up beside a tall adobe fence surrounding a dwelling. Our car lights shined on two large metal gates hanging on sturdy hinges. The gates met in the center of the gateway where they were held together with a heavy chain and padlock. We watched in the car lights as our friend, who had been

driving, walked to the gate and pounded his fist against the heavy metal. In a few moments the chain was unlocked from the inside, and a short man with a dark complexion opened the gate. He was dressed in black pants, a white short-sleeved shirt, and a black tie. After a moment's pause there was recognition, followed by a wide, spontaneous smile and embrace.

We were soon introduced to him, and he invited us into his humble home. As we walked through the courtyard toward the small, humble dwelling, I noted that a new, more commodious home was under construction nearby. We were greeted at the door by a gracious wife. She too was small in stature. Her raven hair hung in long braids, and her dark eyes sparkled as she smiled and bade us welcome. She was a beautiful quiet woman, her countenance clearly depicting her Lamanite heritage. The room we entered was virtually half of their home. It served as kitchen, dining room, and bedroom. We were invited to sit on the edge of the bed. Our hostess soon presented each of us with a half slice of watermelon. It was a welcome, delicious treat to our thirsty bodies. As we ate I noticed our host had not joined with us and inquired why. I was told that he had just returned from a home teaching visit. The family he had visited was facing some challenges, so he was fasting and praying in their behalf. Our conversation turned to his new home and their progress on its construction. We learned that work on the home had been postponed for the past year because their financial resources and time were directed toward helping build their branch building that had just been completed.

"I guess now that the church is finished you will be able to start working on your house?"

"No. You see, a young man in our branch wants to go on a mission, and we will all be helping finance him. Our home will have to wait."

Tears came to my eyes. I glanced around at the humble

surroundings. A small closet held the limited wardrobe for husband and wife. I saw a clean but painfully humble home with no running water, no carpeted floors or soft sofas with matching drapes, no TV or refrigerator, no sink or dish-washer—a home poor in worldly possessions but rich in spirit, a home filled with love sanctified by devotion and sacrifice.

"One day," I thought to myself, "I will want to gain admittance through another gate into the celestial realms on high. I think I will just slip my thumb into the corner of this man's pocket and let him pull me along. When we approach the gate I will smile at the gatekeeper and say, 'I'm with him.' "

Not all important Church jobs or everyday tasks are in the limelight. Indeed, there are many quiet men and women who faithfully perform their daily tasks without much notice. Their part in our lives is vital, yet they seemingly go unrewarded. They do it because it's right and it brings them satisfaction. Perhaps the Lord spoke of them when he said, "For he that is least among you all, the same shall be great" (Luke 9:48).

15

Of Foolish Ventures

Something was wrong with my dog, Spotty. I could tell by the way he was acting. Without his usual bounding, barking, tail-wagging greeting, he slipped quietly like a shadow around the corner of the building.

Sensing his need for my attention, I, too, slipped around the building to learn the reason for his strange behavior. A quick glance told the story. Spotty's face was bristling with white pointed slivers that gave him the look of a grizzled old prospector with a face covered with whiskers. He whimpered pleadingly, rubbed his nose toward the ground, and pawed at his face and lips trying to remove the cause of his pain. A porcupine had driven a multitude of sharp quills deep into his tender nose and quivering flesh.

He saw me now and looked up toward me with pleading eyes as if to say, "I know I have been foolish. I should have known better, but won't you please help me?" He made another futile pass at the cruel barbs protruding from his bloodied face, which merely added to his pain and further proved the hopelessness of his situation.

I walked over to my nearby car, removed a pair of pliers from the glove compartment, and walked back toward him. "This is going to hurt, old fella," I said softly as I carefully pillowed his pain-ridden head in my lap. He looked back at me with limpid eyes as if to say, "I understand."

As I began the painful extractions, I talked to him quietly. I suppose I was talking to myself as much as I was to him. "What would you do without me now, old fella? You are in a rather hopeless situation, aren't you? How would you ever get these quills out by yourself?" He looked directly at me, and I felt he understood. I wondered what would have happened to him if I had not come to his aid. I could imagine those painful barbs finding their way deeper and deeper into fevered flesh. In my mind I could see his face festering and swelling as the pain became so unrelenting that old Spotty would do almost anything to escape from it.

"How like old Spotty we are," I thought to myself. "How many times do we find ourselves in foolish circumstances from which we cannot escape?"

My thoughts carried me to a man kneeling in a garden alone. Upon him was placed the burden of all the sins of the world. The weight of this debt brought pain and anguish beyond our understanding—pain of such magnitude that he, the Son of God, sweat blood from every pore. I thought of my own life, of foolish ventures that brought me sorrow; but because of this man kneeling alone in the garden, I could be spared. Jesus had done for me that which I could not do for myself. My pain could be removed, my tortured spirit healed. I could look up once again with hope and promise.

I could feel old Spotty tremble with pain each time I touched him, but he made no protest. Finally, the last quill was removed from his sad face. I stroked his fevered head gently and felt the warm softness of his fur beneath my fingertips. With painful effort he lifted his head and turned with gratitude to lick my hand.

My thought returned to Jesus long ago. His feet were bathed in tears and dried with the hair of a repentant sinner. I longed to show my love to him, to bathe his feet with my tears, to kneel before him and show my love.

Spotty was all right now. He rose stiffly and walked cautiously away with his tail inscribing small arcs of happiness. We had learned something today, Spotty and I—something for which I am grateful.

16

A Better House

The sun always sank quickly behind the large red hills dominating our little valley ranch in Montana. It was bright and shiny one minute, and twilight, then dark the next.

The chickens sought shelter rather frantically that summer. It was the summer of my uncle's escapade, the summer he tore down the chicken coop. You could see the poor fowl seeking refuge under the willows by the creek or under the boards leaning against the barn. They needed warmth and shelter from the cool nights, but more important they lived in mortal fear of the marauding coyote or bobcat.

It all started with my uncle finding fault with the chicken coop. It was small and crowded. The roof leaked and the door slumped on sagging hinges. It's overall appearance certainly did not enhance the ranch landscape. This bothered my uncle so much that one sunny Saturday afternoon, much to my grandmother's alarm, he tore the old hen house down. He promised to build her a better one. But he never did.

I learned a lesson from this even during those tender years. My uncle meant well, he really did. But he never got around to replacing what he had destroyed.

Until we have demonstrated our ability to improve something we might be well-advised to withhold our judgment. Until we have done better, we might well keep our peace. I feel certain that had the chickens been given a voice, their preference would have been for the old house. Don't tear down another man's house until you have built him a better one.

17

Where Would You Have Him Go?

The story of the prodigal son is a beautiful illustration of love and compassion. The young son, having wasted his inheritance in riotous living, finally in a penitent spirit turned his tired, lonely footsteps homeward. But when he was yet a great way off, his father saw him and had compassion, and ran and fell on his neck and kissed him.

The father placed his best robe upon his shoulders and a ring upon his finger and shoes upon his feet. Then he commanded his servants, saying, "Bring hither the fatted calf, and kill it; and let us eat, and be merry: For this my son was dead, and is alive again; he was lost, and is found. And they began to be merry." (Luke 15:23–24.)

The joy at his return was marred by the reception from his older brother who had remained faithfully behind. This son did not rejoice at the return of his wayward brother;

instead, he was angry and refused to join in the merry-making.

Somehow, he felt that he was being cheated, that his father's joy at this brother's return was a betrayal of his own demonstrated loyalty and faithfulness. The joy that he might have shared with his brother and father was smothered in jealousy.

An interesting question might be posed to the older brother: "Where would you have your brother go?"

If in his weakness he chose to consort with evil companions but now, repentant, he returns home, should we lock our doors against him? Everyone needs friends. If he finds no friends at home, then where will his friends be found? Will we force him to a life of exile and poor companions?

This same question might be posed in a modern setting. Some years ago our family moved to a new location, and it became necessary for each of our children to find new friends. Because of her own pleasant manner, my oldest daughter, Kathy, had always found this to be an easy task. It was delightful to see her circle of friends enlarge as time went on. Then a rather traumatic condition developed in her young life. In her usual way, Kathy had tried to befriend everyone. One of her new acquaintances was a young girl who had been wayward but was trying to return to activity and fellowship in the Church. Unfortunately, the other girls her age had drawn a tight circle that kept her out. As Kathy fellowshipped her "prodigal friend," she found herself being shut out by those who should have come to her assistance and strengthened her in her efforts. More than once, she came to me in tears, saying, "Daddy, what should I do? If I befriend Margaret, the other girls won't have anything to do with me; and if I don't befriend her, she will lose her only real tie to the Church!"

What an unfair and unnecessary choice! Kathy's effort

was heroic in keeping Margaret from returning to her old friends and so to her old ways. A circle was drawn, doors were closed, and all the signs said, "You have sinned, you are not wanted here." How much easier it would have been if a warm circle of love had opened for her, and she had been made to feel the security and strength of being wanted.

There are thousands of persons both in and out of the Church who know loneliness and long to return. They come in many ways, but each is cautious, searching, hopeful of understanding and acceptance.

A number of years ago, we had a very active stake missionary program in our locality. Many new friends were coming to us regularly through the waters of baptism. Some members had difficulty accepting the new converts because they remembered how these persons lived before they accepted the gospel. Things seemed to reach a climax when they baptized "Old Cowboy Tom." People were heard to say, "They'll do anything for statistics. They are only trying for numbers. Why, they even baptized Old Cowboy Tom. Cowboy Tom was well known by everyone. He was past middle age and stood six feet three inches tall in the cowboy boots that were always on his feet. He had owned and operated the local tavern for twenty-five years.

But Tom taught us all a lesson. If a circle was drawn to keep him out, he didn't see it. His emergence from the waters of baptism literally brought him forth into a newness of life. Leaving his old self behind, he formed new habits and found new associations.

As he was found worthy to receive the priesthood, he insisted upon having the blessing of serving in each office of the Aaronic Priesthood. Perhaps the greatest demonstration of humility I have ever observed was to see six feet three inches of Tom's profile standing humbly before the sacrament table with a group of twelve-year-old deacons.

Eventually, he was ordained a teacher and then a priest.

As time passed, and he continued faithful, he was given the Melchizedek Priesthood and soon emerged as a stalwart leader in his quorum and community. When asked why he had waited so long to join the Church, his answer was obvious, "No one asked me. No one ever taught me." You see, we had judged him. We had drawn a circle and kept him out, but he drew an even larger circle that took us in.

The Apostle Paul in counseling with the Galatian Saints recognized the need for members to help one another. He said, "Brethren, if a man be overtaken in a fault, ye which are spiritual, restore such an one in the spirit of meekness; considering thyself, lest thou also be tempted" (Galatians 6:1).

Let us each find room in our hearts to rejoice at the return of our wayward brothers, feeling in our hearts the need to rejoice: "For this my son was dead, and is alive again; he was lost, and is found."

18

Look Not on His Countenance

When I was growing up as a child and we referred to the President of the Church, it had always been "President Grant" for as long as I could remember. I am still embarrassed by my reaction when President George Albert Smith was called to succeed him.

In my youthful judgment, President Smith was not the handsome man that President Grant had been and could not be compared with his counselor David O. McKay, whose manly head was crowned with beautiful snow-white hair. Since I lived away from the center of the Church, I had no way of knowing President Smith except through his pictures which appeared in the newspapers or magazines. Somehow his thick glasses and small goatee beard didn't represent to me the way a prophet should appear.

Imagine our surprise when we learned he was going to attend our stake conference. Most of us had never dreamed that in that remote section of Wyoming we would ever be in the presence of a prophet of God. On that special day the stake center began filling very early and, as expected, soon overflowed into adjoining buildings before the conference began.

We were among the early arrivals, so we enjoyed a good seat among the Saints. I was a teenager at the time, but the memory remains as if it were yesterday. A spirit pervaded that conference with a richness and intensity that made me feel like both laughing and crying—laughing for joy and crying for joy. When President Smith rose to speak to the congregation a spirit of love and power emanated from him and touched me deeply. I found myself sitting on the edge of my chair breathing in his every word.

Indelibly impressed upon my memory is the spirit of his testimony. He concluded his address with words similar to these: "I am an old man. I will not remain much longer upon this earth. I have nothing to gain by deceiving any of you. Knowing this, I want to tell you that I know that God lives. This is his church and God directs it."

As he continued, the spirit of his testimony touched my heart. I felt a warm, spiritual confirmation of the truthfulness of his words. In a way entirely new to me, I felt drawn toward him with a love and reverence I could not explain.

Several months later when I learned of his death, I cried at the loss of a loved friend. His powerful testimony returned in my memory with an even greater conviction. George Albert Smith, my friend, my brother, was indeed a prophet of God.

I learned a lesson at this early age. Physical appearance alone is not an accurate gauge in judging anyone. The Lord taught us that principle many times through the scriptures. In choosing the Lord's anointed, Jesse prepared his sons to pass before the prophet Samuel for his appraisal. In so doing Jesse never even considered showing his youngest son,

David, who was out keeping his sheep. The Lord, however, had counseled Samuel: "Look not on his countenance, or on the height of his stature; because I have refused him: for the Lord seeth not as man seeth; for man looketh on the outward appearance, but the Lord looketh on the heart" (1 Samuel 16:7).

19

The Truth Will Go Forth

It was five o'clock in the morning when the telephone rang. It did not awaken me, for I had scarcely slept through most of the night. It was still dark but the wind-blown snowflakes could be seen through the window pane before they were swept away.

I was presiding over the Arizona Holbrook Mission, and it seemed that every new group of missionaries were transferred to us during the worst weather of the winter. Today was no exception.

As I answered the telephone, a cheerful voice on the other end of the line said, "President, this is Elder Priest. We just wanted you to know that we are all right and we're on the way. We are in Page, and the other couples are traveling together with us in a caravan. I have a four-wheel drive, and we'll be fine. Not to worry. We'll see you later this afternoon."

I replaced the receiver trying hard to hold back tears of

relief. Having missionaries young and old scattered over four different states and living in often remote areas was a tremendously worrisome burden, especially during blizzard weather conditions. The additional worry over arriving and returning missionaries in the midst of this was almost overwhelming.

I have often reflected upon this singular experience. Here it was in the middle of winter. Road conditions were terrible. Ice and snow were everywhere, the wind drove the chill from the cold air into the marrow of your bones, and yet . . . "Not to worry, President, we are on our way." The mission had been in place for many years. The first missionaries had visited this area more than one hundred years before, yet there was an urgency that drove this work forward even in the middle of the year's worst snowstorm.

This example nearly always came to my mind when I would stand with the missionaries at our zone conferences and recite in unison the Standard of Truth as written by the Prophet Joseph Smith in his Wentworth Letter:

> The standard of truth has been erected; no unhallowed hand can stop the work from progressing; persecutions may rage, mobs may combine, armies may assemble, calumny may defame, but the truth of God will go forth boldly, nobly, and independent, till it has penetrated every continent, visited every clime, swept every country, and sounded in every ear, till the purposes of God shall be accomplished, and the Great Jehovah shall say the work is done.

20

Clogged Machines

One cold winter day we could be seen working around our clogged hay grinder, loosening bolts and pulling tightly compressed alfalfa from its interior. There wasn't anything really wrong with the grinder—it was just that Herman was insensitive. As soon as we could, we would replace him. He had plugged the machine just one too many times.

Grinding hay was a noisy, dusty job reserved for the winter months when time was more abundant and when the cattle were in the feed lot.

This task required a crew of several men. It was usually a cold winter day when we crawled up on the stacks, frosty pitchfork in hand. The tractor would be coughing black smoke rings and powering the large pulley which drove the long belt extending to the grinder. It was an invigorating exercise to feed the hungry grinder on one end and distribute the chopped hay pouring from the other end into the receiving truck or wagon.

Since it took several of us to perform this task, we sometimes traded help with the neighbors in order to have a full crew.

One particular neighbor would sometimes offer to help, but as soon as we could we would find someone else. As we fed hay into the grinder, we would each instinctively listen to the rhythm of the laboring tractor motor. Occasionally, an extra large forkful of hay would slow the speed of the grinder, and the tractor motor would labor to recover its speed. When this happened, we would pause long enough for the motor to recover and the revolutions to increase before we resumed. Somehow, our neighbor was insensitive to this whole procedure. The grinder would slow almost to a halt, groaning under its burden, but he would keep right on pitching hay. Sometimes he would look over toward us with a questioning glance wondering why we had stopped, leaving him to do all the work. Several times, the tractor motor completely stalled, and we had the laborious and time consuming task of unplugging the grinder. Our neighbor meant well, but he was insensitive.

How often in our everyday lives are we like that erring neighbor, insensitive to the sounds around us?

The hour is late, the meeting has been long, and it is nearly time to dismiss; but we are asked to bear our testimony. Do we now proceed to give a lengthy sermon or, in effect, continue pitching hay into a faltering machine?

We are on the same program with a visiting authority, and time is short. Are we sensitive enough to shorten our remarks in consideration of his message?

You are visiting friends. They are glad to see you, but you come unannounced and they are not prepared for company. Do you greet them and make a polite exit, or do you linger longer?

Someone at the office teases a fellow worker. It becomes obvious that this is a sensitive issue and taken personally, not to be joked about; but we go right on teasing. Are we not stuffing hay into a clogged machine?

There are few qualities that are more greatly to be desired than sensitivity. Becoming sensitive to the feelings of others and to the world around us requires one to think beyond himself and to consciously consider how others might feel. Perhaps this is what the Savior had in mind when he said, "Whatsoever ye would that men should do to you, do ye even so to them" (Matthew 7:12).

21

The Boy Is Worth More Than the Cow

It seemed as though he had just pulled the covers over himself when his father called, "Cal! Get up! Time to be up and about! Get your chores done. I'll be in from the field in about an hour and then we'll have breakfast."

Cal heard the door close as his father stepped out into the morning darkness. Fighting the desire to curl back under the warm covers, he rolled to the edge of the bed and dropped his feet onto the cold floor. His eyes strained against the darkness as he reached near the foot of his bed and picked up his soiled Levi's. The mud from yesterday's labor in the field still clung to them. They were cold against his shivering body as he stepped into them. His bare feet were feeling around the floor for his stockings while he buttoned his Levi's.

An overwhelming self-pity swept over him as he located his stockings. They were caked with the sweat and dirt of several days and holes were widening in them in several places. He guessed there were clean ones around somewhere, but he sure didn't know where they were and he hadn't taken time to look.

His feelings of self-pity persisted while he worked the soiled socks over his cold feet.

Nobody cares about me! he thought to himself.

"Mother has been gone for more than two weeks now. If she cared anything for me, she wouldn't go off and leave us just because some lady is having a new baby. All Dad cares about is the crops or the pigs or those darned milk cows! If he's so fond of cows, why doesn't he milk them himself instead of making me do it?" Thus his thoughts continued while he groped his way cautiously toward the front door. The sharp morning air quickly drew the drowsiness from him.

Cal gathered up the milk pails from the shed and started toward the barn. He kicked a bucket lying in his path and sent it banging and whirling across the barn yard. This gave vent to some of his emotions, but his mood was still sullen.

"All Dad has to do is start up that old tractor and sit there while I do all the work! I have to haul the grain, pitch the hay, slop the hogs, and milk these darned old cows. Those cows had better not try anything this morning!" He said to himself, "If Belinda so much as raises her foot she'll really get it!"

As he crossed the corral, his horse, Dan, nickered from the shed and came trotting out to meet him. Cal broke open a bale of hay and kicked part of it toward the hay manger.

"That will take care of you, you old nuisance."

By the time Cal had fed the pigs, filled the water troughs and milked most of the cows, the sun had risen and was shining brightly. It warmed his back as he started milking the last cow, Belinda. He always saved the long milkers till last hoping that one day his father would step over the rail and say, "Hold it, Cal. I'll finish up for you."

"Fat chance that that would ever happen. Dad doesn't care about me. All he cares about is these darned cows."

The pail gave off a sharp ring as he forced in the pure white slivers of milk. Soon the sound softened as the rich milk, foaming white and fragrant, began to fill the pail.

Cal was nearly finished when he heard a voice. It sounded like Old Man Jones was here again. He was probably pestering Dad to sell him Belinda. He could hear Mr. Jones's voice rising above that of his father. They were standing on the other side of the milk shed, and Old Man Jones was saying, "I don't know why you are so stubborn, Harry! Why don't you want to sell me that cow?"

His father was quick to reply, "Because a man doesn't go around selling his best cows when he's trying to build up his herd. That's why, Elmer!"

Old Man Jones had pitched his voice to a shrill squeak that drowned out all other sound.

"If she's such a good cow, Harry," he squeaked, "then why do you let the kid milk her?"

Cal stopped milking. The silence seemed eternal while he listened for the reply.

"Because," his father spoke in a firm, quiet voice, "the boy is worth more than the cow."

Maybe it was the morning sun shining down on Cal's back, or perhaps it was the thoughts of his mother coming home soon, but, somehow, he felt warm all over. He gave one final tug on Belinda, tossed the milk stool toward the fence, picked up the milk pail, and strode briskly toward the house.

He was whistling his favorite tune.

22

Only What You Give Away

We were surrounded by excitement when my uncle returned from his Tongan mission. Three years is a long time to be gone, and in my tender years my memory of him was dim. I knew him mostly from the colorfully stamped and wrinkled letters that came regularly. There were occasional photographs of him in his white shirt and white pants, with palm trees in the background that fired my imagination. After being carefully passed around for all to see, the pictures were placed in a position of prominence upon the mantle. Sometimes Grandmother received a battered package smelling of mothballs or carrying the musty, damp smell of the islands.

My uncle's homecoming was a great family affair. We were all very proud of him.

A huge, weathered trunk laden with the mysteries of the islands was carried into our large living room. The lid sprang open when unfastened, revealing a bright array of colorful *lava lavas*, sea shells, grass skirts, *tapa* cloths, wooden carvings, beaded necklaces, *kava* bowls and all sorts of romantic memorabilia.

Soon chairs were pushed back and throw rugs moved to the corners of the living room. A huge, elaborately ornamented brown and white *tapa* cloth was spread out in the center of the floor. We were then seated in a large circle with our bare feet tucked under our folded legs. An exciting chant was given in the Tongan tongue, and we soon joined in. My uncle expertly pounded *kava* in the huge wooden bowl, straining it in a practiced way. After an elaborate ceremony, the half-shell coconut *kava* bowl was finally passed, first to my grandfather and grandmother and then to my mother and father. Eventually, it even came to us lowly children to taste of its bitter, numbing contents.

With this and other ceremonies completed, my uncle began in earnest to unpack his gift-laden trunk. He was lavish in his generosity. My sisters each received grass hula skirts strung with real seashell bands, and necklaces to match. My heart pounded when he handed me a beautiful, sleek, hand-carved canoe. Its tapered sides were ornately carved and etched in white, the outriggers securely fastened with coconut fibers. Small wooden oars made it complete. There were many other handsome gifts, with apparently no one forgotten.

In the years that followed, the precious trunk, which still contained many treasures, was stored in the back room of my grandmother's house while my uncle was living away from home.

One evening, as the school bus dropped us children off near our home, we were astonished to discover our grandparents' house was gone. Nothing was left of the proud, old wooden frame house but smoldering ashes and wisps of smoke. An electrical short in the attic while no one was home had resulted in the destructive fire and total loss of property. Many irreplaceable family photographs, records, and treasures were permanently gone. With a shock we remembered my uncle's chest from the islands. It was only ashes. He had taken none of these things with him.

Several weeks later, most of us almost spontaneously came up with an idea: we would return to him many of the gifts he had given. My boat was a treasured possession on my dressing table, but what fun it was now to be able to give my beloved uncle a gift in return.

Soon his home with his new wife was filled with treasured memories of his mission. He had many beautiful objects, but all he had was what he had given away. The few things he had kept for himself were gone forever.

Our lives are much like this. Really, the only things we take with us are those things we give away.

23

I Stand at the Door

I glanced at the clock. The luminous hands shining through the darkness indicated it was 11:00 P.M. The telephone had awakened me, and it continued to ring; so I lifted the receiver and said, "Arizona Holbrook Mission."

"President Lynn?"

"Yes."

"President, we have a problem and need your counsel."

"I'm listening."

"President, we have been teaching this family—a man, his wife, and several children. There has been a lot of dissension in the home along with other problems that were happening before we started meeting with them. They have been trying hard lately to improve. We have been teaching them the discussions, and they have become very interested in learning about the gospel. Tonight, after we left their home and returned to our quarters, we were just retiring for the night when our phone rang. It was the father of the family calling us in a very excited voice asking us to come help them. He said there were evil spirits in his home, and he wanted us to come make them leave.

"My companion and I prayed together and in a spirit of faith drove up to their home. As soon as our car lights shined against their windows, the front door opened and we were ushered inside. When we entered the home, a dark, oppressive, foreboding spirit enveloped us. Exercising our faith, we commanded these spirits to depart in the name of Jesus Christ. Our faith was rewarded, for we could immediately perceive a different spirit in the home. They thanked us sincerely and we left and returned home. We had scarcely entered our quarters when the telephone rang again. It was the same family calling and more alarmed than before. 'After you left,' they told us, 'the evil spirits returned even worse than they were before. Please come back again.' President, can you help us? What should we do now?"

I pondered for a moment before responding. "Elder, it is not enough to cast out an undesirable spirit, thus leaving the home empty. You must replace it with something better. You must invite the Spirit of the Lord into the home. Do you have your scriptures? Turn with me to Matthew, chapter 12, verses 43 through 45." So we read together:

> When the unclean spirit is gone out of a man, he walketh through dry places, seeking rest, and findeth none.
>
> Then he saith, I will return into my house from whence I came out; and when he is come, he findeth it empty, swept, and garnished.
>
> Then goeth he, and taketh with himself seven other spirits more wicked than himself, and they enter in and dwell there: and the last state of that man is worse than the first.

"President, how do we replace the bad spirit? How do we invite the Spirit of the Lord into their home?"

I have thought about this question often. It is a very relevant question for each of us: How do we in our day-to-day lives invite the spirit of the Lord to be with us both individually and as a family?

Again I pondered before responding. "Elders, I would suggest several things for you to consider. First of all, be very positive and cheerful in your conversations and interactions with the family. I would suggest that you select several appropriate hymns and sing them together with everyone participating. I would further suggest that you take turns reading from the scriptures and sharing with each other faith-promoting stories and experiences. Bear your testimonies to one another. Express your love to one another, and, most important, pray. Ask the Lord to be with you. Invite him into the home. Make him feel welcome."

It was reported to me later that this became a sweet experience for all concerned. There was no further need to command the spirits to depart. A spiritual climate was created in that home that left no room for evil spirits, and they departed of their own volition.

As I reflected upon my experience with the Elders, I realized in retrospect that I had described what could have been a family home evening.

We have a painting hanging on the wall of our office depicting the Savior standing in front of a door to a home. The Savior is poised, ready to knock on the door. This door is different than most doors, however, for on the outside it has no doorknob. It must be opened from the inside. It suggests what the Lord has told us: "I stand at the door and knock." It also suggests that *we* must open the door, if it is to be opened, and invite him in.

Wisdom suggests that we not only invite the Spirit of the Lord into our lives but also carefully avoid those things that will entice evil spirits.

We can, through poor choices and actions, drive the Spirit of our Heavenly Father from us. For example, the Book of Mormon tells of a period when the Nephites chose wickedness, and "the Spirit of the Lord did no more preserve them . . . because the Spirit of the Lord doth not dwell in unholy temples" (Helaman 4:24).

Transgression can and will drive the Spirit from us just as will a spirit of contention. The Spirit of the Lord cannot dwell in rich abundance where quarreling and bickering are the order of the day or where there is serious transgression. The Spirit of the Lord is not invited when raucous music blares and indiscriminate television viewing is practiced. However, when we seek with a spirit of humility, love, and obedience to do those things which would invite his Spirit, we may become as the people of King Benjamin's day who could claim, "Because of the Spirit of the Lord Omnipotent, which has wrought a mighty change in us, or in our hearts, that we have no more disposition to do evil, but to do good continually" (Mosiah 5:2).

Perhaps the best tool the Lord has given us for maintaining our spiritual health is the scriptures. Elder Bruce R. McConkie has told us that "men will be denied the sweet whisperings of the Spirit that might have been theirs unless they pay the price of studying, pondering, and praying about the scriptures" (*Ensign*, May 1986, p. 81).

24

If the Trumpet Give an Uncertain Sound

The class was dismissed. Boys and girls gathered their books with their usual youthful chatter. They left the seminary singly or in groups, their eyes and interest focused on their next activity.

Alone now, I slumped rather wearily into my chair at the front of the classroom, perhaps a bit discouraged and certainly distraught. Today had been especially trying. I had played center stage in a recurring scene with Dennis.

He had challenged nearly everything I had said about the gospel. He had resurrected for reexamination some questions I thought we had put to rest in previous discussions. Several times he had skillfully forced me into a position

Taken from the *Ensign*, Wayne B. Lynn, March 1981. Copyright © 1981 The Church of Jesus Christ of Latter-day Saints. Used by permission.

where I had to take a stand. I had once again borne testimony to the truth of the eternal principles I was teaching and had added my own personal witness.

Now, sitting at my desk, I began to wonder if on some things I had been too firm, too dogmatic. Certainly, I had taught the Church position supported by scripture, by the Brethren, and by my own personal experience. But had I been so firm that youth could not accept? Would I lose boys like Dennis or girls like Alice, who sometimes took his part?

I was prayerfully pondering this question as I began straightening my desk at the front of the classroom. John, one of the students, stopped by to collect some books he had left behind.

"How ya doin'?" he asked.

"Fine, John. How are things with you?"

"Great! I enjoyed your class last period, even if Dennis did lead us away from the lesson for a while."

John was a little cautious as he framed his next question. "Does it bother you when he challenges what you say and takes the negative side?"

I quietly admitted that it did, but that my real concern was my apparent inability to reach Dennis and convert him to a more positive attitude of faith in the Lord's teachings.

John smiled. "I thought you felt that way," he said. "Let me tell you something about him.

"Dennis has many friends who are not members of the Church. He seems negative here in class, but when he gets over to high school, he becomes you! The arguments he gives in class are the arguments he gets from his friends. The answers you give him are the answers he gives back to them. He's just storing up ammunition."

John picked up his books and smiled a good-bye. I sat down again at my desk, smiling. Suddenly everything fell into place. When Dennis asked questions in the future, I would understand. I would be glad to help him find answers.

Then a fear swept over me. What if I had faltered? What if I had compromised? I would not have won Dennis over— I would have betrayed him and the sacred trust of being his teacher.

It was the Apostle Paul who said, "If the trumpet give an uncertain sound, who shall prepare himself to the battle?" (1 Corinthians 14:8.) We don't blast the trumpet in someone's ear, but neither do we indiscreetly sound its message; rather, the call should be sweet and sure and certain of sound.

25

The Pay That Doesn't Come in an Envelope

The task of teaching, particularly in the Church and especially with young people, may be a most challenging and thankless task on the one hand and a most rewarding and eternally enriching one on the other. Often the rewards for our efforts are slow in coming or may not be recognized as quickly. This is especially true with teaching. With this in mind, I share this personal experience.

"Some of your pay will be the kind that doesn't come in an envelope," the seminary supervisor had said. Five years later, as I walked through the doors of the holy temple with heart overflowing, his words were recalled again in sweet memory.

The assurance given years before had been realized

many times, but today was special. To appreciate this moment, we must go back more than five years to a teacher struggling within himself to decide whether a seminary assignment should be accepted in lieu of employment offering greater financial advantage. Perhaps the intimation of "the kind of pay that doesn't come in an envelope" tipped the scales toward a decision in favor of the seminary assignment.

Events leading up to this beautiful experience in the temple began on one of those days when my mood matched the dismal weather outside. That day, a sharp wind was carrying bits of paper and debris in a snake-like procession down the trash-strewn alley and past the doorstep, where it lodged in an ugly pile against the woven wire fence. Skies overhead were dark and threatening, and to me the whole world seemed gloomy.

I stood looking out of the spattered kitchen windows, where a light rain made small wet spots that were quickly blown over with loose dirt. Even the dirty windows matched my darkened feeling. This was not a good way to feel, and I battled against it. Moving to the desert sands of Arizona was a change in itself from the green mountains and water-filled streams of the section of Wyoming that was home to me.

Released-time seminary had been granted there that year for the first time, and President William E. Berrett had counseled the local brethren to start holding released-time classes immediately.

Time did not permit the construction of a building. The first day of seminary, classes were held in a Boy Scout bus parked on the vacant lot that hopefully was to be the site for our new building. Those who have traveled with young boys can imagine the condition of the bus—a somewhat different situation from the commodious classrooms and office to which I had been accustomed.

Forces of opposition had seemed to battle our every step

in trying to rent a building for seminary purposes. Houses were promised, only to be withdrawn when pressures from outside sources became too great. The second week of school had begun before we succeeded in renting a small frame house—a very humble dwelling next to the alley and opposite the high school. Kitchen cupboards soon became library shelves; cabinets were full of student journals; the small living room became our classroom; the single bedroom became an office; and a duplicator was precariously perched on a bathroom shelf. We stacked paper supplies in the bathtub with fingers crossed, hopeful that no one would turn on the water.

In the town, rumors and controversy, surrounded by exaggeration and misunderstanding, greeted our new program of released-time seminary. Although efforts were made to calm troubled waters, little was added to the popularity of the new seminary teacher who had become a symbol of the controversy.

So here I stood at a spattered window, looking out at the clouded skies and trash-filled alley and asking myself if it was worth it.

My reflections were short-lived, however, as a group of energetic students soon arrived and began crowding into the improvised classroom. Chairs were rapidly filled, and little space was left for the teacher.

Knowing that a teacher must be happy in order to succeed with his class, I cast off my gloomy spell and launched into the lesson with as much enthusiasm as I could possibly muster. I was rewarded with appreciative interest and participation by most of the students—that is to say, all of them except the back row of senior boys, who leaned back in their chairs and issued an unspoken challenge for any teacher to reach them.

Following class discussion, I gave a reading assignment in their text, the Book of Mormon. The boys on the back row were slow to open their books, and I noted that one did not respond at all. His book lay unopened on the arm shelf of his chair while he looked at me as if to say, "Just try to make me like this class!"

My gloomy mood returned in spite of my efforts, and I again asked myself, "Is it worth it?" Then I made a very conscious resolve. That young man with the unopened book, whom I will call Jim, would answer this question for me. "All right, Jim, old kid," I said to myself, "you will be my measuring stick. I won't give you any special attention above other students, but I will use you as a gauge of my success or failure. If I fail to reach you, then I will have the answer to my question." This unspoken pledge was important to me in the days that followed, but it was pushed to the back of my mind with the pressures of everyday tasks.

Classes continued, and our old building began to be looked on with tolerance and growing fondness in spite of its inconvenience.

In the meantime a conference with the high school principal provided me with insight into the challenges I faced with some of my students. I was particularly concerned about the senior boys. When I mentioned Jim's name, the reaction was electric.

"Let me show you something," the principal said, stepping to his file cabinet.

After a brief pause he pulled Jim's file from a drawer, opened it, and began reading a few comments that had been submitted by various teachers: "Drunk and disorderly at the school dance." "Profane and abusive language directed at the teacher." "Disrespectful and rebellious toward authority."

"I would like to see you reach that kid!" was the principal's comment, and I wondered again at the task I had set for myself.

As weeks passed, I became much closer to my students,

and strong bonds of friendship were formed through spiritual experiences we shared in class. Then, several months after the beginning of school, I almost unconsciously became aware of some changes in Jim's attitude. The book on his desk, which had long remained unopened, was finally being opened and read with interest. He began to ask questions and participate in class discussions.

Several little incidents reflected Jim's change in attitude, but one stands out above the rest. It was the day we talked about contention. Our lesson was structured around the counsel given by the Savior:

"For verily, verily I say unto you, he that hath the spirit of contention is not of me, but is of the devil, who is the father of contention, and he stirreth up the hearts of men to contend with anger, one with another" (3 Nephi 11:29).

I had previously arranged with one sometimes-rowdy student to assist me with an object lesson demonstrating the bad feelings we have when there is a spirit of contention. With my permission he deliberately came into class late, banged down his books, and sprawled out in his seat without apology.

In anger I snapped at him, "What's the big idea? Why are you late? I don't like your attitude one bit!"

Indignantly, he shouted back, "Well, I didn't ask to take this class!"

I retorted in kind. "Well, we can get along without you!" Whereupon he gathered up his books and angrily stomped out of the room.

A quietness filled the classroom until Jim's spontaneous comment broke the silence, "Oh, for Pete's sake, Harold, come back here and act your age!"

We had a lot of fun that day bringing Harold back into class and reestablishing order. We talked about how terrible we felt when there was a spirit of contention in the class, but the thing we most remembered was Jim's comment and his obvious desire to be a part of a good seminary class.

Skies seemed brighter after that day. My days were often made easier when I overheard comments by students, such as, "Have you noticed the change in Jim lately? The boys he buddies around with say he won't even take a drink anymore."

One day a senior boy lingered behind after class and said, "I have something to tell you that you might be interested in. You know, part of my home teaching assignment is to go with my companion to Jim's house. Well, the other night when we were there my senior companion was talking to Jim's parents, and the old subject of taking time from school for seminary came up again. Jim's mother rather forcefully said, 'I'm against it myself; I don't think they should mix church and school.' Then she turned to Jim and asked, 'What do you think, Jim?' Jim looked at her and said, 'Mother, it is the greatest desire of my heart to become a seminary teacher.' His mother nearly fell out of her chair!"

Jim never spoke to me about any of this, but his humble spirit told me much more than words could express. His decision to live according to the Lord's way was also a strong influence on his friends who followed his example. There was even talk about Jim's desiring to fill a mission. Students told me that he had decided to attend college for one year, preparing himself to serve the Lord as a missionary.

The following winter I received a letter from Jim, who was away from home attending the university. By that time we had moved into a beautiful new seminary building, located on the same spot where we had parked the bus only a year before. We had left our rented house near the alley with an emotional farewell.

Jim's letter brought a lump to my throat: "I don't know how to thank you . . ." He poured out the feelings of his heart in a way that he had been unable to do in person. "I have come a long way," he continued. "I watched you all

year and waited for you to make a mistake." This frightened me! Then came his request: "I don't know if they have
told you, but next month I leave for my mission. Will you
speak at my farewell?"

Today as I drove through the early morning darkness to
the temple, my thoughts returned to Jim. I thought about
the mission he had honorably filled, and the sweet young
girl he was about to marry. I thought about all the other
youngsters who had presented such a challenge and had
become so special to me. My soul filled with warmth as I
remembered that every senior boy that year had now completed an honorable mission for the Church. Many were married, as Jim was being married today, in the house of the
Lord. They were fine young men with whom he associated;
and like him, I called them my "sons."

The temple ceremony was beautiful. Clothed in white,
the couple knelt at the altar and exchanged vows of eternal
love and devotion.

As I walked from this beautiful house of God, I tasted of
the fruit of being a teacher. I had taken a large bite of "the
kind of pay that doesn't come in an envelope," and it was
delicious.

Index

—A—

Accountability, 21–22
Adversity, opportunity through, 40
Arizona Holbrook Mission, family
    encounters evil spirits in,
    85–87
    missionaries in, 74–75

—B—

Bank loan, payment of, 19

—C—

Cancer, Joyce Jensen's courage with,
    40–42
Charity, 48
Chicken coop, torn down, 65–66
Commitment, 7
Contention, illustrated in seminary
    class, 96–97
    Spirit of the Lord driven away by,
    88
Courage, example assists gaining of,
    33
    not fighting back as demonstra-
    tion of, 48
    speaker's demonstration of, 50–52
Cowboy, dragged by horse, 3–4

—D—

Dance, fight at, 45–48
David (King), 72–73
Discouragement, 40
Dog, wounded by porcupine quills,
    62–64

Drugstore, story about honesty in,
    9–10

—E—

Elders. *See* Missionaries
Elementary school, fire drill at,
    12–15
Evil spirits, 85–87
Example, courage learned by, 33
"Expectations in Spring" (poem),
    41–42

—F—

Faith, 7
Farm, milk cow on, 79–81
Fear, 7
Fight, boy challenged to, 45–48
Financial sacrifice, 55–56, 59–61
Fire, keepsakes destroyed in, 82–84
Fire drill, 12–15
Free agency, 22
Friendship, importance of, 68–69

—G—

Gifts, fire's destruction of, 82–84
Guidance, divine, 29

—H—

Hay grinder, and insensitive neigh-
    bor, 76–77
Honesty, 9
    seminary class tested on, 10–11
Horse, cowboy dragged by, 3–4

—I—

Ice fishing, spiritual guidance during,
    23–29
Indian boy, paralyzing accident of,
    33–39
Innocent people, negative association
    hurts, 18
Insensitivity to others, 77–78

—J—

Jensen, Joyce, story about, 40–42
Jesus Christ, suffering of, 63
    on contention, 96
    knocking on door, 87
Judgment, learning to withhold, 66
    physical appearance not criterion
    for, 71–73

—K—

Kites, analogy of, 53–54

—L—

Love, 68–70

—M—

Marriage, 7
Mexico, church members in, 59–61
Milk cow, and young milker, 59–61
Missionaries, attacked by rowdy
    drinkers, 48–49
    in bad weather, 74–75
    evil spirits banished by, 85–87
Missionary, fire destroys keepsakes
    of, 82–84
    paralyzed Indian boy as, 36–39
Mistakes, 4

—O—

"Old Cowboy Tom," baptism of,
    69–70

—P—

Parachute jump, and letting go, 5–6
Paralysis, of Indian boy, 33–39
Peter (Apostle), 7–8
Physical appearance, not criterion for
    judgment, 71–73
Porcupine, quills in dog, 62–64
Preparation, required for success, 16
Prodigal son, modern analogy, 67–68

—R—

Recording studio, visit to, 20–21
Released-time seminary, experience
    of teacher in, 93–98
Relief Society lessons, written by ter-
    minally ill sister, 40–42
Restraint, 54

—S—

Sacrifice, financial, 55–56, 59–61
Seminary class, boy's questions in,
    89–91
    honesty test in, 10–11
    progress of boy in, 94–98
Sensitivity to others, 77–78
Shoshone Reservoir, fishing at, 23
Skunk, girl who smelled like, 17–18
Smith, Don, cheerful paraplegic,
    33–39
Smith, George Albert, boy's judgment
    of, 71–72
Smith, Joseph, on standard of truth,
    75
Speaker, courage shown by, 50–52
Spirit of the Lord, must be invited,
    87–88
Stake conference, George Albert
    Smith at, 71–72
Stake dinner, financial sacrifice at,
    55–56
Stake missionary program, 69–70

Stake priesthood meeting, speaker at, 51–52

Standard of truth, Joseph Smith on, 75

Still small voice, 30

Success, 16

—T—

Teaching, 92

Temptation, 21

Tongan Mission, missionary returned from, 82–84

Transgression, 88

"Trial of Your Faith, the" (Relief Society Lesson), 41

—U—

Unpleasant tasks, 18

—V—

Volunteer fire department, and hypothetical fire, 13–15

—W—

Warning, from the Lord, 29

Wheelchair, Indian boy confined to, 33–39

—Y—

Young girl, peers' rejection of, 68–69

Young man, courage in speaking assignment, 50–52